BONNIE PRINCE CHARLIE
AND
THE JACOBITE REBELLIONS

INTRODUCTION

When he sailed into Loch Shiel in a small boat, with a small band of supporters, he was a young man on a mission.

It was 11a.m. on 19 August 1745. Stepping ashore at Glenfinnan, was Prince Charles Edward Stuart, son of the Old Pretender, James Francis Edward Stuart and grandson of the late King James II, VII of Scotland. He was Bonnie Prince Charlie. His quest? To win back the Crown for the House of Stuart. His supporters became known as the Seven men of Moidart.

Expecting to be greeted by a gathering of the clans, Charles was met by some 150 Macdonalds of Clanranald. It was an inauspicious start for the Prince who had left France fully expecting to mount a successful military campaign to restore the Stuarts to the British throne.

Eventually they arrived, sufficient men to make the raising of the Standard of the House of Stuart worthwhile. The Old Pretender was declared King and Charles his regent.

So who was the enemy? King George II! And why was the restoration necessary? The "Glorious Revolution" of William of Orange and his wife Mary, daughter of King James II, who were crowned King William III and Queen Mary II at Westminster Abbey on 11 April 1689. James II was deposed.

On the death of William III in 1702, he was succeeded by his sister-in-law Queen Anne, followed by George I and George II.

Had James II still been in power when he died in 1701, the Crown would then normally have passed to his son James. However the forced abdication of James II, followed by The Act of Settlement of 1701, made sure that George Louis, Elector of Hanover and great grandson of James I was crowned King George I.

The Act which allowed only a Protestant succession, was based on the premise, that, since the Reformation of the Church, Catholics were incapacitated from becoming the monarch. The opinion was that Catholics accepted the Supremacy of the Pope and could not, therefore, Swear the Oath of Allegiance and intend to keep it.

There was also the argument that countries such as France, Spain and Portugal would no more admit a Protestant successor, than Sweden or Denmark, a Catholic. The exclusion based upon religion was not peculiar to the throne of Great Britain and Ireland.

Although excluded from the succession, Prince Charles and his father nevertheless considered themselves to be Charles III and James III, thus becoming known as the Pretenders.

The only option available was to fight
- thus we have James, the Old Pretender and the Jacobite Rebellion of 1715
- followed by Bonnie Prince Charlie and the rebellion of 1745.

The Glenfinnan Monument, erected to commemorate the raising of the Jacobite Standard. The statue at the top was modelled, on a Jacobite supporter in error, not Prince Charles.

JAMES II

MARY OF MODENA

THE DEPOSED KING AND HIS QUEEN

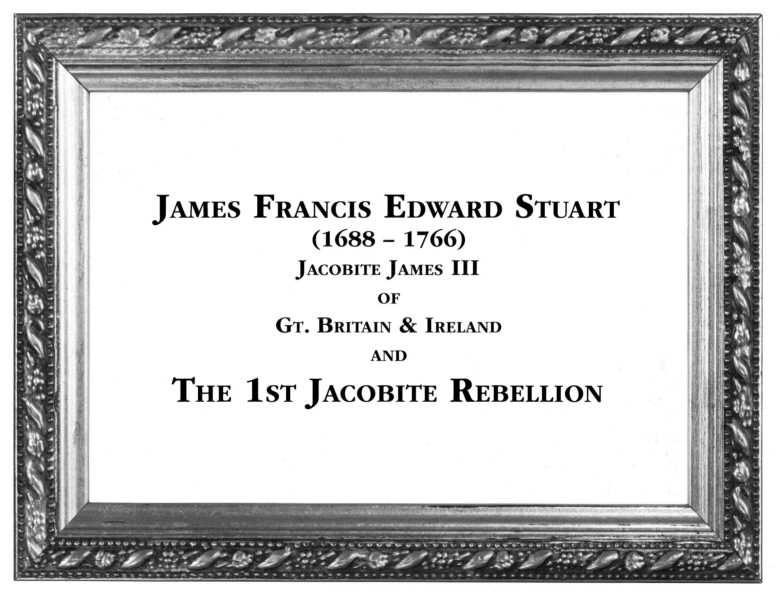

James Francis Edward Stuart
(1688 – 1766)
Jacobite James III
of
Gt. Britain & Ireland
and

The 1st Jacobite Rebellion

THE 1ST JACOBITE REBELLION

It was the birth of his son James Francis Edward Stuart to Mary of Modena, the second wife of James II that triggered off the removal of James II as King and his replacement with joint sovereigns William III and Queen Mary II.

As stated in the introduction had James II still been in power at the time of his death the Act of Settlement of 1701 would have prevented James Francis Edward from succeeding him. It also meant that he could not succeed Queen Anne.

Even before Anne's death in 1714 her leading officials had already been scheming to undermine her and place the Old Pretender on the throne. Both Robert Harley (Earl of Oxford) and Henry St John (Viscount Bolingbroke) were involved.

Shown opposite is a document which links the two officers. It is a Treasury Warrant signed by Harley as Earl of Oxford (1661-1724) – leader of the administration (1711-1714) for the payment of salary at £1,850p.a. to Bolingbroke as Secretary of State for South Britain, 28 May 1714. Queen Anne dismissed Harley in July 1714 because of his contact and correspondence with the Jacobites and he was locked in the Tower of London between 1715 and 1717.

Only one of Anne's pregnancies had survived for any length of time. Prince William, Duke of Gloucester was born in 1689. Although not a healthy child his death in 1700 came as a shock as he was expected to become King.

After Anne died George Louis, son of Sophia youngest daughter of Elizabeth, daughter of James VI, became King as George I, Sophia having predeceased Queen Anne leaving George to become King.

When George became King there were over fifty descendants of James I with a better claim to the throne than he had.

Elizabeth of Bohemia

The Elizabeth referred to in the narative above is Elizabeth of Bohemia as she was the Queen of Frederick V of Bohemia. Shown here is Elizabeth's signature from a letter she sent to Elizabeth, the wife of her secretary, Sir Albertus Morton.

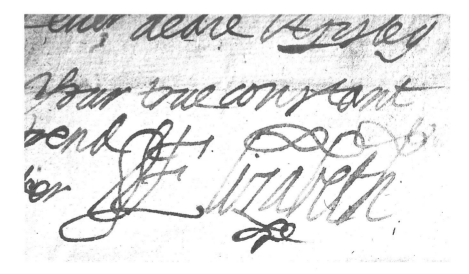

After my hearty Comendacons By vertue of her Ma:ts Letters
of Privy Seal bearing date the 31.st day of October 1710 These are
to pray and Require your Lordship to draw an Order for paying
unto my very good Lord Henry Lord Viscount Bolingbroke, one
of her Ma:ts Principall Secretarys of State, or to his Assignes, the
Summe of Four hundred sixty two pounds, ten Shillings, for one
Quarter of a Year due at Lady day 1714 On his Lop. Allowance
or Sallary of Eighteen hundred and fifty pounds p Anni And
Let the said Order be satisfied Out of any her Ma:ts Treasure or
Revenue being and remaining in the Receipt of the Exchequer
applicable to the uses of the Civill Government For which This
shall be your Lordsp. Warrant Whitehall Treary Cha:rs 28.th May 1714.

To my very good Lord Cha. Lord Halifax
Auditor of y:e Receipt of her Ma:ts Exchequer

Oxford

5

George I (1660 – 1727)
The Rebellion begins.

George I ascended the throne on 1 August 1714. He was crowned on 20th October 1714 and the 1st Jacobite rebellion started in September 1715 when at Braemar, John Erskine, 6th Earl of Mar raised the standard declaring James Francis Edward Stuart, Jacobite James III (VIII of Scotland) as King.

After successfully capturing Perth and Inverness the Jacobites under Mar met up with the King's troops under the 2nd Duke of Argyll at Sheriffmuir on 13 November 1715. Sheriffmuir is an area of moorland near to the Cathedral city of Dunblane in Stirlingshire. Although the battle is regarded as having been a stalemate it was really a Jacobite failure as far as the succession to the throne was concerned.

The Old Pretender did not arrive from France until December 1715 and soon fled back to France with the Earl of Mar.

Monuments at Sheriffmuir

The 1st Rebellion was a non-event as far as the succession is concerned but not in relation to casualties.

Shown opposite are two monuments erected at the Sheriffmuir battlesite, a large one by the Clan Macrae Society in memory of the members of the clan who fell almost to a man – and a small one by the 1745 Association. The monuments were erected in 1915 on the two hundredth anniversary of the battle.

PLAYER'S CIGARETTES

GEORGE I

George I

MONUMENTS AT SHERIFFMUIR

THE BATTLE OF SHERIFFMUIR

On this moor on 13 November 1715, a Jacobite army composed largely of Highlanders under the command of the Earl of Mar met a Hanoverian army consisting mainly of regular British soldiers under the Duke of Argyll, at what has become known as the Battle of Sheriffmuir. The result was indecisive but Mar's failure to take advantage of Argyll's weakened position in the closing stages of the conflict and subsequent withdrawal from the field contributed to the failure of the Rising - known as "The Fifteen" - in favour of the restoration of the exiled King James VIII (the "Old Chevalier").

ERECTED BY THE 1745 ASSOCIATION

The Clan Macrae Society   *The 1745 Association*

The 6th Earl of Mar

This letter had been sent by Mar on 10/10/1710 to the Earl Marischal of Scotland. The Earl had supported Queen Anne and the Treaty of Union in 1706/7 before he and the recipient came out for the OLD PRETENDER. The Earl Marischal was George Keith (10th Earl) who continued to support the Old Pretender in exile.

Mar gives Keith an update on events in London and a meeting he and some others had with Queen Anne and how he hopes that when the Duke of Hamilton and the rest of them return to Edinburgh they will continue to agree with each other.

The Queen was desirous that they would do so. He also comments on the fact that he and Keith had always been on the side of the Cavaliers and he was ready and willing to continue along the same lines. He hopes that none of those who had recently disagreed with them would succeed in dividing them just for their own particular benefit.

The historic role of the Earl Marischal of Scotland was to protect the Royal Regalia of Scotland and the sovereign when attending Parliament. Mar was the Governor of Stirling Castle.

My Lord

I'm very glade yr lop: is recoverd of yr in=
=disposition & I hope very soon to be merrie wt you. I wou'd
have wrote to yr lop: long ere now, had not resolutions of our
bussiness been so long a takeing at London, by its being so late be=
=fore twas knowen what parts some people wou'd take at this
juncture, It was but the day before I left London that the Queen
spoke to some of us togither & I hope when the Duke of Hamilton &
the rest of us come to Edr we shall continue to agree togither as
her Majestie was pleased to recomend to us. Those of us who wish the
support of the monarchie have now an opportunity in our handes to
put it pritty much out of hazard & thereby recomend our selves to
the Queen, who I'm perswaded will be very reddy to give those who
do so all due incuradgment. If we do not divid amongst our selves
we cannot well miscairie & I hope we of that principle will be
wiser. Yr lops familie & mine have alwayes been on the Cavalier
side & for my shair I'm resolved to continue so, as I'm perswaded yr lop:
is. When I come to Edr: I'll be very wiling & reddy to concert mea=
=surs wt yr lop: & I hope afairs may be so ordred that non of those
who have at this time stated themselves in opposition to us, by not
likeing the measurs lately taken, will prevaile that no body who chance
to be angrie upon their own particular account will be able to
break or divid us. Since I did not write to yr lop: from London I
cou'd not refrain from doing it now, ther's no body whatever more

E. Marishall

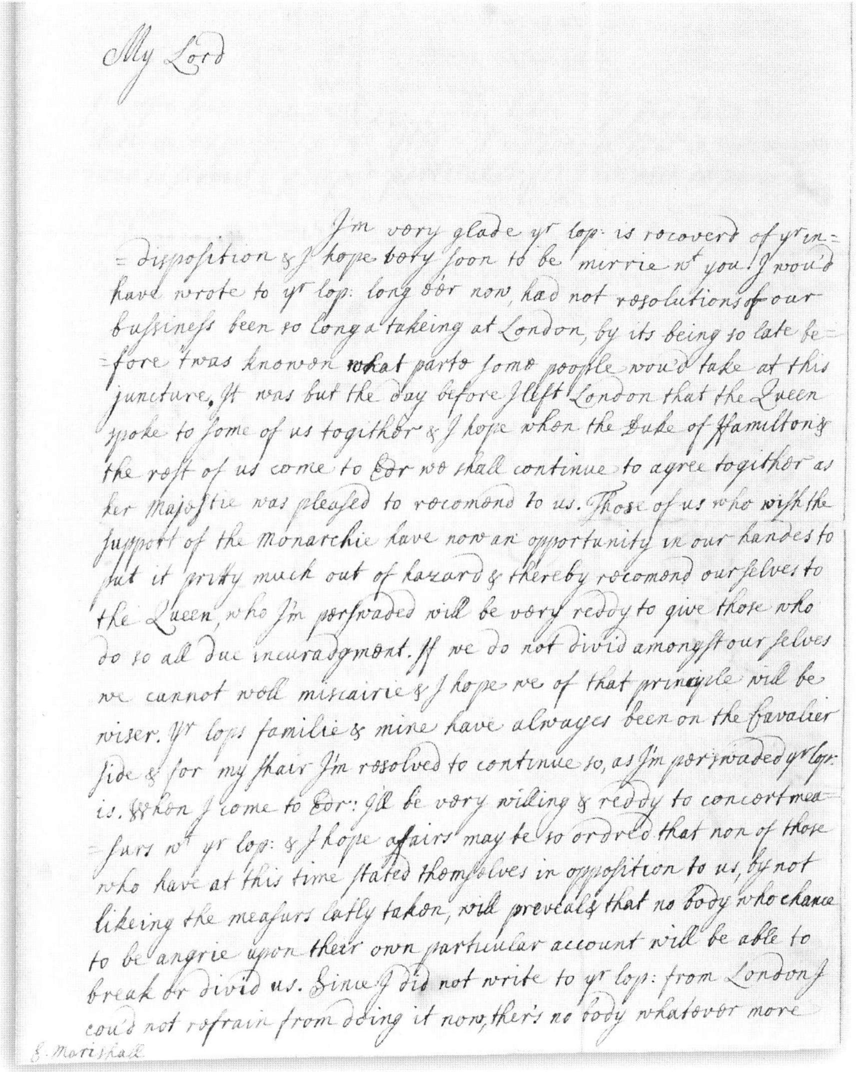

The Earl writes to the Earl Marischal (two pages)

yr lops humble servant nor wishes better to yr familie & if ever it be in my power I wou'd esteem it my honour as it is my inclinations to forveit & yr lop in particular, for I am with all sincerity & respect

My Dear Lord

Yr lops most affectionat cousin & most faithful humble servant

Mar

MAR'S WARK

One of the consequences of Mar's defeat at Sheriffmuir was the forfeiture of the family's estates. Although his brother managed to buy back the estates later this did not include the right to reside in Stirling Castle.

Mar's Wark had been in the family since it was built by John Erskine (1510-72) the 1st Earl, first hereditary keeper of Stirling Castle and 1st Regent of King James VI.

John Campbell the 2nd Duke of Argyll and Duke of Greenwich was George I's commander in chief in Scotland and in charge of the government forces in the Rising. He was one of the Commissioners who negotiated the Union of the Parliaments and was one of the first two officers of the British Army to be promoted to Field Marshall. There is an elaborate monument in his honour in Westminster Abbey.

A son of the 1st Duke the 2nd Duke wrote a series of letters to his lawyer Ronald Campbell in Edinburgh in 1704. This two page letter signed "Argyll" and dated 11 November 1704, from London is featured in Patricia Dickson's "Red John of the Battles". In the letter the Duke complains about delay in receiving £1,000. The letter says "If I havena that £1,000 with the answer of this letter and am not for the future pay'd, surely to a day I shall alter my method for by God Allmighty I will not starve for the saik of my Family or anything on earth." He also threatens to "sell and make myselfe easy that way."

At Inveraray the Eleventh day of August One thousand seven hundered and fifteen years —

Which day Conveened within the Tolbooth of Inveraray The ffreeholders and other Iheretors within the Shire of Argyll particularly afternamed In Obedience to the circular Letters sent to them by the Justice Deput of Argyll (Acquainting them of ane Invasion designed by the Pretender upon His Majesties Dominions and desireing them to meet this day and place to Consert proper Measures for the Service of the Government and Securing the peace of the Country) They are to say

Dugald Lamont of Inverine
Sir Neil Campbell of Ellangreg
Sir John Campbell of Carricks
Coll Alexander Campbell of Ffinab
Colline Campbell of Strathohurr
Mr John Campbell of Otter
Angus Campbell of Donnstuffradge

Robert Melvile of Kilmichael
Duncan Lamont of Fetchinghelloch
Coll Lamont of Innermilbeg
James Lamont of Knockdow
Duncan McGibbon of Achingarren
Charles Campbell of Ballochneil
Patrick McArthur of Trivadich
Alexander Campbell of Sondachan

Shown here is the first part of a resolution signed at Inveraray on 11 August 1715 in support of King George and against the intended invasion. The letter was signed by a long list of Freeholders and Heritors of Argyll and what is noticeable is the overwhelming number of Campbells signing the document.

LETTER FROM PRINCE GEORGE TO THE 2ND DUKE OF ARGYLL

Prior to the battle of Sheriffmuir and after the foregoing resolution the following autograph letter in French was sent to the 2nd Duke of Argyll by Prince George, then the Prince of Wales and signed "George P". In this letter, St James's, 17 September 1715 he promises to do his best to persuade his father, George I, to send reinforcements to Scotland, clearly in preparation for the rebellion.

St James's ce 17. Sept. 1715.

J'ai appris avec chagrin, MyLord, par votre lettre du 15. la mauvais disposition où vous avez trouvé vos Troupes en Ecosse. Je ne l'ai point attendu pour tâcher de persuader le Roy à Vous envoier du renfort. Mais je n'ai pas pû en venir à bout jus, ques à aujourd'huy, où le Roi a enfin consenty à envoyer Evans pour vous emmener son Regiment d'Irlande. Je crois que les Avis que Vous recevons de toutes parts, et qui conviennent tous, qu'un soulevement nous menace en ce pais cy ont empêché un renfort plus considerable. Les mesures que vous avet prises pour sourier d'Edinbourg et pour mettre Perth hors d'insulte ont eté fort approuvées. Le comman= dement de cette premiere place, avoit d'ja eté donné à Preston, lequel est party il y a dix 2 jours pour s'y rendre. Et Dieu mon cher Duc, soiet persuadé de mon estime, et que ne remarque, fai jamais d'occasion pour l'ou marquer mon amitié.

George R.

Inveraray Castle, Argyll

13

George I appoints a Lieutenant Colonel before Sheriffmuir

By this Commission, signed at St. James's George I appoints Lewis de la Boiragon to be a Lieutenant Colonel in Morrice Nassau's Regiment. The document is countersigned (bottom right) by James Stanhope, 1st Earl and Viscount, dominant minister from 1714 to 1721

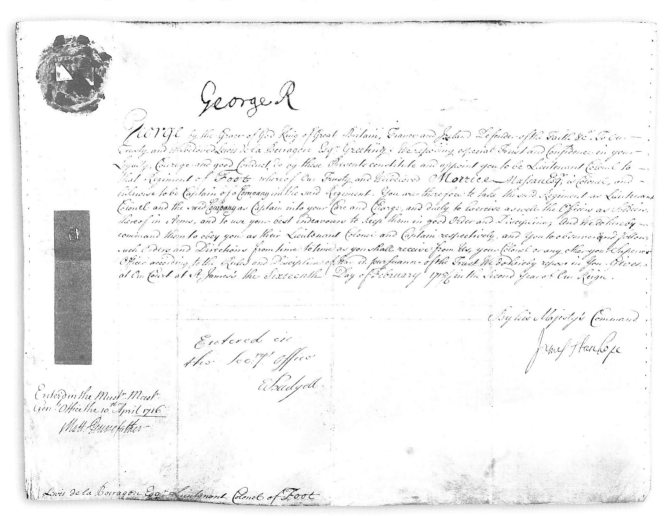

MARY OF MODENA WRITES TO CARDINAL ODESCALCHI

Although James II had died in 1701, Mary of Modena survived until 1718. In the attached letter of 27 February 1716, not long after the rebellion failed Mary writes to her cousin, Cardinal Odescalchi concerning a recent festival and appreciating his friendship. His friendship was undoubtedly of importance to her at this time, just three months after her son's defeat.

Mon Cousin, Les tesmoignages de Votre zele que
Vous me rendez à l'occasion des dernières festes
me sont tres agreables, et j'y suis d'autant plus
sensible que j'estime beaucoup Votre amitié, et
Que je me fais un plaisir de vous assurer que je
Suis avec les sentimens d'une parfaite gratitude,
Mon Cousin, à St Germain en Laye le 27e
Fevrier 1716

Votre affectionnée Cousine
Marie R.

PUNISHMENT & RETRIBUTION

The Scottish Clans supporting the Old Pretender and Lord Mar included the MacGregors, Macleans, Macdonalds, Lord Lovat Clan Fraser and the Gordons. The Whig Clans supporting King George and Argyll included the Sutherlands, MacKays, Rosses and Munroes and some of the Frasers. After the rebellion hundreds of Jacobites were sent to the Plantations, there were executions; peerages and estates were forfeited.

THE EARL OF DERWENTWATER

The border clans supporting the Old Pretender included Derwentwater and Forster south of the border and Kenmure on the Scottish side. The 3rd Earl of Derwentwater and Viscount Kenmure were executed on Tower Hill in 1716. Derwentwater was a cousin of The Old Pretender, his mother being a daughter Moll Davis had to Charles II. He was brought up in St.Germain with James Stuart, the Old Pretender.

Shown opposite is a historic document dated 9 December 1718 being the settlement by the Commissioners appointed to sell the seized estates of the traitors involved in the 1715 Rebellion. The document awards a considerable amount to Richard Dashwood a Norfolk claimant written in English on three sheets of vellum with a striking calligraphic heading indicating that the hearing was held at Essex House in London and the Commissioners were George Treby, Sir Thomas Hales and Henry Cunningham with John Bath Sergeant at Arms with the fine signatures of the three Commissioners and the Royal wax seal against each signature.

The document includes property and money in Lancashire belonging to the Earl of Derwentwater, a most respected man caught up in events. One of the most picturesque lakes in the Lake District bears his name. Keswick is but a few minutes walk from Derwentwater. It's oldest coaching inn, the George Hotel is shown here. On his way to the Rebellion the Earl of Derwentwater, who lived on Lords Island on the Lake, called at the George to quaff a tankard of ale from the saddle.

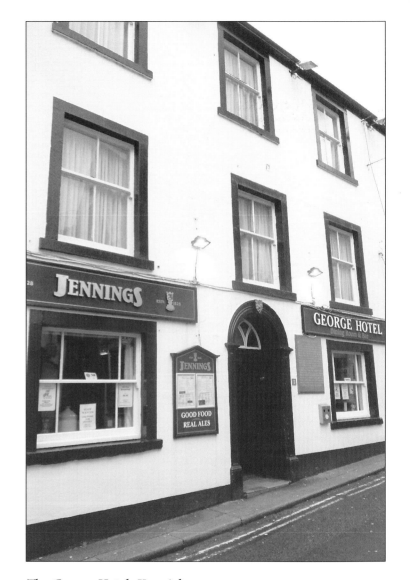

The George Hotel, Keswick

The Commissioners sell off the Estates of Traitors

Derwentwater, Cumbria

THE 4TH EARL OF TRAQUAIR

Charles, the 4th Earl of Traquair, was another ardent Jacobite supporter of the Old Pretender. He was involved in the 1715 rebellion. Between 1697 and 1711 he and his wife had seventeen children. Their son, the 5th Earl, also a Jacobite was imprisoned in the Tower of London following the 1745 rebellion. His wife volunteered to join him.

Traquair House, (shown here), Innerleithen in Peebleshire, is reputed to be the oldest inhabited house in Scotland. Guests here have included Mary, Queen of Scots and Bonnie Prince Charlie. In direct contrast to the open arms extended to Mary and Bonnie Prince Charlie, the Earl of Traquair lent a deaf ear when during the Civil War the 1st Marquis of Montrose hammered on the door, seeking refuge after his defeat at the battle of Philiphaugh.

JAMES, THE OLD PRETENDER

Shown here is page 1 of an autograph letter sent by the Old Pretender soon after the rebellion, initialled, Urbino, 13th December 1717, in French to an unnamed recipient referring to his situation in exile, the welcome he has received in Italy saying that it is not his fault that he is still not married, then continuing to talk about the nature of his conduct towards a Count, how the people of Italy are solid and reasonable, and while in Rome he learned of things that were being done on his behalf which humbly touched him, looking forward to receiving news of the addressee's family which is so dear to him, etc.

Since the death of his father King James II in 1701, James Stuart spent most of his life in exile, mainly in France. The death of Queen Anne in 1714, prompted him to believe a rising might suceed. The Treaty of Utrecht in 1713 quashed this idea with France supporting the Hanovarian succession to the English Throne. The King of France was Louis XIV. Spain also recognised the Succession. The Prince therefore travelled south into Italy and took refuge with the Pope. As a more permanent residence he moved to the Ducal Palace at Urbino, where the Prince spent his time dreaming of his hoped-for succession to the English throne.

Letter from the Old Pretender 13 Dec, 1717

JAMES MARRIES CLEMENTINA

James was in Spain in 1719 when an unsuccessful rising took place in the Highlands. Marrying the Polish Princess Maria Clementina Sobieski by proxy in May 1719, James returned to Italy the following September for the formal ceremony.

THE BIRTH OF CHARLES AND HENRY

In 1720, Charles Edward, Bonnie Prince Charlie was born, followed by his brother Henry Benedict who later became Cardinal York.

CLEMENTINA AND MRS DILLON

Here is a letter, in French, written to Mrs Dillon, and signed "Clementina R" as Queen Consort of King James III Rome, 2nd November 1733. The Queen states that she has received her correspondent's letter thanking her for the help she had shown Mrs. Dillon's son, the Count of Malta. In a lengthy postscript she refers to her correspondent's daughter, 'I rejoice with all my heart, as you do, at your daughter's decision to take the veil as a nun, even though you will have felt this separation deeply. I am convinced that her new life will one day be of great consolation to you..... I have at heart everything which concerns her, and she deserves nothing less from me'. Autograph letters of Sobieski are rare following her early death at the age of 32.

The marriage of Clementina and the Old Pretender was an unhappy one and they separated. Despite a reconciliation, Clementina eventually became a recluse and died in 1735.

Clementina writes to Mrs Dillon

JAMES WRITES TO MONSIEUR CARRARA

Another letter sent by The Old Pretender is this one, dated 22 July 1754, from Rome. In the letter to Monsieur le Chevalier Carrara, James thanks Carrara for his compositions which he will look at in his spare time and assures him of his respect.

JAMES DIES

James died in 1766 and was buried in St Peter's in Rome, being joined later by Princes Charles and Henry. Their marble tomb was paid for by King George III.

Monsieur Le Chevalier Carrara. J'ai receû votre Lettre du 22. Juillet et les exemplaires de vos compositions que vous m'avez envoyé pour Les quelles Je vous remercie, et Je me ferai un plaisir de les regarder a mon Loisir. En attendant Soyez bien persuadé de mon estime, et de La Consideration que J'ai pour vous. Sur ce Je prie Dieu, qu'Il vous ayt, Monsieur Le Chevalier Carrara, en Sa Sainte garde. A Rome ce 21. Aoust 1754

Votre bon Amy

Jacques R;

"ROB ROY" MACGREGOR (1671 – 1734)

Robert MacGregor

Famous outlaw & cattle thief

Jacobite supporter, 1715

THE PERSECUTION OF THE CLAN GREGOR

In 1603, King James VI issued an edict proclaiming the name McGregor to be abolished. This followed years of inter-clan battles and killings. From 1603 the Clan would be persecuted by law and anyone with the name and refusing to renounce it would be put to death. To be a McGregor was illegal until the edict was repealed in 1774.

Despite the edict, McGregors were still being supported in the Highlands, much to the chagrin of the Privy Council so much so that in 1611 a commission was passed ordering the holding of regional courts for the purpose of making examples of those disobeying the law and ensuring sentences were both passed and carried out.

Rob Roy of the outlawed McGregor clan, livestock dealer, cattle thief and outlaw often masquerading as a Campbell was the colourful Jacobite who acted as guide for the rebel army at Sheriffmuir. He took no part in the fighting but was charged with treason and spent his later years as a fugitive. He also captured Falkland Palace in 1716.

Rob Roy was born Robert MacGregor in Buchanan Parish in 1671 to Donald MacGregor (15th Chief of the MacGregor Clan) and his wife Margaret, daughter of Campbell of Gleneaves - hence giving good reason for Rob Roy's use of the surname, Campbell. In contrast to his appearance Rob Roy was literate and educated. Indeed history informs us that many members of his family made a name for themselves in various walks of life - and not as rascals.

The McGregor clan had lost lands in the early 14th century when it was given by Robert the Bruce to the Campbells and lost the remainder in the 15th and 16th centuries. A force of clansmen fought with the Marquis of Montrose for the royalists. Charles II repealed the edicts outlawing the McGregors but William of Orange re-imposed them. Rob Roy lost his lands to the Marquis of Montrose having defaulted on a debt.

Before the rebellion of 1715 Rob Roy was a figure often seen in Inveraray despite the fact that there were Wanted Notices for his apprehension. The 2nd Duke of Argyll gave him shelter although Rob Roy supported the Old Pretender and the Duke led the King's troops.

THE LAW – A MANUSCRIPT LICENSE OF 1619

The persecution of the Clan Gregor was so severe that it was even forbidden to communicate with clan members. Shown opposite is a manuscript license dated 1619 granted to Duncan Campbell of Glen Orchy giving him permission to "intercommune" with certain members of Clan Gregor, signed by Alexander Seton, the Lord Chancellor of Scotland (1604-1622) as A. L. Cancell.s and James Primrose, clerk to the Privy Council. Provenance – Sir Duncan Campbell of Glenorchy (1546 – 1631) "Black Duncan of the Cowl" and subsequently part of the Breadalbane papers.

BLACK LETTER ACTS OF 1716

Following each Jacobite rebellion several Acts of Parliament were passed. They were known as Black Letter Acts.

Details of two of these Acts relating to the first Jacobite rebellion are shown below. The purpose of the Acts was primarily to deal with the Jacobites.

The two printed black letter Acts of parliament were passed on 20/2/1716 - the first requiring "papists" to register their names and real estates and the second being the Act of Pardon for the Jacobite rebels who took part in the 1715 uprising. This Act was an amnesty to the Scots involved but excluding "all and every person and persons of the name and clan MacGregour".

The covers on the two Acts are identical. One is shown.

Black Letter Act 20/2/1716

Forsamekle as sume ordour and coursf being now in handis for sup-
pressing of the barbarous and rebellious thetis and Lymmaris callit
the Clangregor wharin all sould prolue ad forw ...
Tharfor the Lordis of Secret counsell gvis and grantis Licence to ...
Sr Duncane Campbell of Glenvrquhy Knight to confer deale and ...
and intercommoun with suche of the Clangregor as he sall think mete
for draving of thame fra the rest of thair follous and making of
thame gif it be possible to tak advantagis ane of another within
pane or danger to be incurrit to the said Sr Duncane Heirthrow in
his persone or goodis Exonering and relesing him of all pane and
danger that he may incur tharthrow ...
the 20 of August 1619.

A.L. Cancell:

LETTER WRITTEN AND SIGNED BY ROB ROY MACGREGOR

Shown opposite is a letter written and signed by Robert MacGregor or Campbell commonly called Rob Roy MacGregor to Baillie Buchanan, chamberlain to the curators of Buchanan of Arnprior, 22 May 1718. The letter is signed "Ro: Roy", an exceptionally rare form for him to use as virtually all Rob Roy's known letters and contracts bear his formal signature "Ro: Campbell. The letter has been backed at some stage and docketed as "Letter from Rob Roy to Baillie Buchanan". It is believed to have been kept in Buchanan family papers from it's date of receipt until it's first sale in 1987. The text of the letter is as follows:

Dear Sir

There is one Patrick Cotter that ingag-l ed himself tennent with me for the l fourth pairt of Corriecheirrich in l febry. last and l am informed now l that he is ingaged tennent in Airdcheil l Rynaerugie so that l hope you being l Chamberland to Arnprier and a man l that l trust very much unto l hop you l doe me the favour as [to] send your l officer to him and [put?] him out of l your bounds for l have no will that l there should be anything that could be l a groudge betuixt us that was so unjust l to me that he never came or sent to me l to tell me that he had altered his l resolution l hope ye will not put me to l the trouble as to write to any other of l the Curators send answer of this l to Duncan McIntyre in Innerchernach l who will faithfully transmitt it to me this l is what should be done betuixt neighbours l and especially [p] as trusts to others as the one l of us does to the other expecting you will del with him l out of your Ground very soon l remain as formerly l Maij 22nd 1718

Sir

yours as formerly

Ro: Roy

BACKGROUND

It seems unusual for Rob Roy to ask for the removal of a cotter when he seems well capable of arranging this for himself.

It is possible that the dispute is part of a long running struggle involving the great powers, the Dukes of Argyll, Atholl and Montrose and the Earl of Breadalbane.

The lands of Corriecheirrich let by Rob Roy to Patrick Cotter belonged to Breadalbane whereas those of Rynaerugie belonged to Montrose.

What is clear is that letters from Rob Roy are extremely rare.

1745

It is interesting to note, that at the time of the '45 rebellion not only were Rob's sons involved but so also were the Buchanans of Arnprior.

Robert Buchanan, (Duke of Perth's Regiment) son of Baillie Buchanan was killed at Culloden.

Patrick Buchanan, (Duke of Perth's Regiment) brother to Arnprior was captured at Carlisle and later discharged.

Francis Buchanan of Arnprior was executed in October 1746.

Rob Roy writes to Baillie Buchanan

Rob Roy, the legend

The word "legend" is used to describe a mythological figure, a character with supernatural powers. Rob Roy earned this status.

When King George IV came to Scotland in 1822 he was accompanied to the Theatre Royal, in Edinburgh by Sir Walter Scott to see a play – 'Rob Roy' – written by Sir Walter.

The MacGregor Clan claimed descent from Kenneth MacAlpine, the first King of a united Scotland. Did the MacGregors feel superior to the Stuarts? – a reason for their failure to conform?

It was John, 1st Earl of Breadalbane, a slippery character, who gave the lands of Corriecheirrich in tack to Rob Roy in 1713. Having had his house burned down in April 1716, Rob Roy returned to Inversnaid. Six months latter his house at Craigrosten was also burned down. Retiring to a house in Glen Shira, on the Argyll lands, Rob appears to have remained there unmolested despite being forfeited for his part in the rebellion.

In his Letter of 1718, Rob may have been particularly annoyed at 'Patrick Cotter' because he defected from Breadalbane's lands to Montrose's Rynarugie. Although no one with the name of Patrick Cotter has been traced among the tenancy records of Breadalbane there is the distinct possibility that "cotter" was a description and not a surname.

Rob Roy, of course, had not always been at loggerheads with Montrose, who had funded his cattle dealing activities, the export of cattle on the hoof to England. Herds were driven south of the border, fattened and sold, thus enabling the sponsor and drover to make profits.

With the name of MacGregor proscribed many of Rob's surviving letters are signed 'Ro: Campbell,' Bonds registered in his name describe him as 'Rob Roy Campbell of Inversnaid' or 'Rob Roy Campbell in Glengyle'.

The Trossachs and Balquidder is Rob Roy country. How fitting it is to find the 'Rob Roy Story' at the Scottish Tourist Board's visitor centre at Callander.

Rob Roy dies

When he died in 1734, Rob Roy was buried in Balquidder church yard.

Shown overleaf is Inversnaid Hotel on Loch Lomond. Nearby is Rob Roy's cave.

William Wordsworth summed up Rob Roy very well.

William Wordsworth & Rob Roy

Excerpts from Wordsworth's poem:-

A famous Man is Robin Hood,

The English Ballad – singer's joy!

And Scotland has a Thief as good,

An Outlaw of as daring mood,

She has her brave Rob Roy

Then clear the weeds from off his Grave,

And let us chaunt a passing stave

In honour of that Hero brave!

———————

Heaven gave Rob Roy a dauntless heart,

And wondrous length and strength of arm:

Nor craved he more to quell his Foes,

Or keep his Friends from harm.

———————

Balquidder churchyard – buried here are Rob Roy MacGregor, his wife Mary, second son Coll and youngest son, Robin Olg (the latter hanged in Edinburgh for the abduction of a young widow)

Inversnaid Hotel – Rob Roy's cave is to the left.

Ben Lomond – Rob Roy Country.

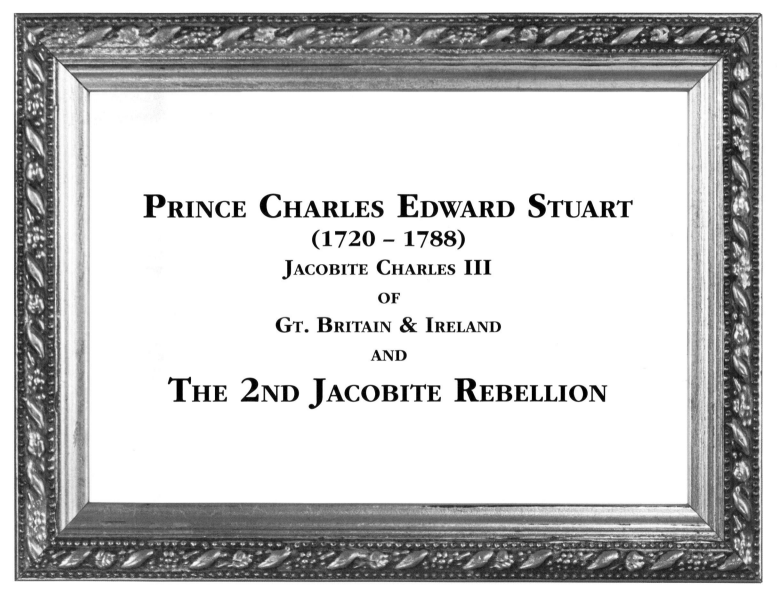

PRINCE CHARLES EDWARD STUART
(1720 – 1788)
JACOBITE CHARLES III
OF
GT. BRITAIN & IRELAND
AND

THE 2ND JACOBITE REBELLION

Bonnie Prince Charlie

The second Jacobite rebellion was led by Charles Edward Stuart – "Bonnie Prince Charlie" - the Young Pretender.

As indicated earlier Charles was born in Rome in 1720, son of James Francis Edward Stuart, The Old Pretender and grandson of King James II of Britain and VII of Scotland.

Charles was a charismatic figure and the last hope of success for the Jacobite cause. His popularity in Scotland is legendary despite his failure in his quest to regain the throne

Down through the centuries religion has been a major factor in events affecting the monarchies of Scotland, England and the United Kingdom.

The adherence of Mary Queen of Scots to her Roman Catholic faith was a major factor in her downfall and execution and although other factors were also present the execution of Charles I was largely due to his similar allegiance and a belief that he had a Divine Right to rule.

In the case of James and his son Charles it was religion that excluded them from the throne.

The rebellion began on 19th August 1745 when Charles raised his Standard at Glenfinnan at the head of Loch Shiel. Accompanying Charles, was a small band of supporters who came to be known as "the Seven Men of Moidart". A simple monument marks his arrival.

In the hills of Lochaber high above the monument is an equally well known scene – the Glenfinnan Viaduct – over which the "Hogwart's Express" has trundled – in several Harry Potter films.

Given the tactical failures during the rebellion, it is perhaps not too surprising to learn that even when the statue at the top of the Glenfinnan monument was modelled, it was not on Prince Charles, but on one of his supporters.

With little significant opposition Charles gathered supporters captured Perth, and entered Edinburgh taking up residence, as Regent, in Holyrood Palace but failing to capture either Stirling Castle or Edinburgh castle.

The monarch at this time was King George II.

Charles's intention was to march to London with a view to claiming the crown for his father.

Note: Although the Prince did not manage to capture Stirling Castle, the Castle run by Historic Scotland, did manage to capture the hearts of readers of Which? who in 2012 voted it the UK's favourite heritage attraction, beating off opposition from the Tower of London and the Houses of Parliament. A fantastic achievement!

George II

At Perth, the Prince stayed in the Salutation Hotel, now the longest established hotel in Scotland (1699). He had room No 20. Stirling Castle, however, he failed to capture in either 1745 or 1746.

THE BATTLE OF PRESTONPANS & SIR JOHN COPE

The first important battle of the rebellion was at Prestonpans on 21 September 1745and this was a decisive victory for Charles over Sir John Cope who was Lieutenant – General, Commander of King George's forces in Scotland. A memorial in the form of a cairn was erected close to the battle site. This relates to all the soldiers who died.

No group of autograph letters by Sir John Cope had been sold separately at auction in over thirty years until three letters came up at Bonhams in March 2011.

All three letters signed ('Jno. Cope'), were to Lieutenant- General Thomas Fowke ('Dear Fowke'). One of the letters is shown here.

The letters are sending news of national affairs ('…The eyes of all Europe are upon our Affairs in America, which 'tis imagined will draw consequences in this part of the World, for which wee are so formidably prepared, by our natural strength, the Navy, that if Spain will but continue to think according to her old proverb, peace with England & War with all the World, so far only, as to keep herself neuter, expressing his desire (with a tacit reference to his unpopularity after 1745) to continue to lead a life of ease …I am just as desirous not to be employed, as those who could employ me are unwilling to do it, so in that we are perfectly agreed…"), reporting that he hears well of Fowke's Governorship of Gibraltar etc thanking him for sending him a fine Spanish horse and for remembering his son [John, a diplomat], and mentioning 'Mr paymaster Pit' and Lord Harrington all with autograph endorsements by Fowke, St James's Place and Bath, 1753-1755.

There is a paucity of knowledge about Cope's life after his Court of Inquiry in 1746. After he was defeated at the Battle of Prestonpans in 1745 he was the subject of the Jacobite song 'Hey, Johnnie Cope! Are ye waukin yet?'

The Memorial Cairn 1745

S.t James place
July 5.th 1753.

Dear Fowke.

I had not yours Letter till Saturday night, I am glad to find by yours that the place and company at Chiltenham are agreable, and have great hopes, that by the Waters not disagreeing with my Lord, that he will reap great benefit by them. I reckon his Lord.ts stay will not be much longer, this, if the Waters are of benefit, and the place tolerable, it is to be wished he may give the Spaw a fair tryal. The Late Rains have put Petersham into great beauty, Mr Stanhope has company with him almost every day, is well, and in good spirits, Mr Cary is much out of order, and from apprehensions of being worse, his spirits are low. The Town is as empty of company as ever I knew it, I make a visit to it for a couple of days, and travel short jaunts into the country. I have business here which requires my looking after every now and then.
Cap.t Fleming was married yesterday to a niece of the present Duke of Somerset, he settles 1000. p.r Ann.m I would willingly send you something to entertain you, but I hear nothing, and my invention is not very good: Scarborough is so full that people of fashion are forced to lye in Garrets. Some of the Rioters at Leeds have by

the civil Magistrates orders been fired upon and killed by a party of Hawly's, a party of 100. of my Regiment is marched to Bradford near Leeds upon the same account.
I ask'd yesterday of M.rs Villar's Servant after her health, he said she still continued ill, she kept her bed.
I have been to make the Divine. M.rs Fitzgerald a visit in the Country, a pretty place when graced by the owner of it: I have not heard any thing of Military affairs since I see you, so what can I say more? than my respects & compliments to my acquaintance at Chiltenham. M.rs Metcalf is well and returns you her compliments for inquiring after her. pray let me hear from you.

I am
Dear Fowke
J.r s
In. Cope

Pray tell M.r Blair that
I will thank him soon for
the favour of his Letter received
yesterday.
My best services to M.rs Fowke.

Sir John Cope writes to Lieutenant General Thomas Fowke.

This large monument was erected to Colonel Gardiner a government soldier who was fatally wounded. The monument was erected at Bankton House where he lived. Close to the battlefield, this house was used as a hospital for all the wounded, both Jacobite and Redcoat. "To Col. Gardiner who fell in the Battle of Prestonpans"

Bankton House, used as a hospital for Jacobite and Redcoat soldiers.

After the Battle

When the battle took place the Redcoats were no match for the Highlanders. While Sir John Cope was making for the safety of the barracks at Berwick his troops were being taken prisoner and marched to Edinburgh. There the Highlanders celebrated their victory. Cope's store of military hardware was discovered and removed from Cockenzie House.

Cockenzie House, where Cope stashed his military hardware.

How many Redcoats escaped by boat from Seton Harbour?

THE LONG MARCH SOUTH
BONNIE PRINCE CHARLIE AT JEDBURGH, ROXBURGH

After success at Prestonpans, Charles continued to march towards London. On 6th and 7th November 1745 he lodged in Blackhills Close, in Jedburgh.

In 1935 the Jethart Callants Club erected a tablet to mark the occasion, the tablet being unveiled by the Duke of Atholl. K.T.

In addition to early Scottish Kings and Bonnie Prince Charlie the town has a remarkable record of prominent visitors. These include Mary, Queen of Scots, Robert Burns and William Wordsworth.

Jedburgh Abbey dominates the town. It was founded by David I in 1138 and Alexander III was married there in 1285.

Also in the vicinity are the remains of Melrose and Dryburgh Abbeys. All three are managed by Historic Scotland. Robert Bruce's heart is buried in Melrose Abbey and Sir Walter Scott is buried in Dryburgh Abbey.

Sir Walter Scott (1771 – 1832) studied law and was an advocate before becoming a major literary figure. In addition to "Rob Roy" to which reference has already been made, Sir Walter wrote "Redgauntlet" the theme of which is an imaginary third Jacobite rebellion, which Prince Charles returns to lead. At Sir Walter's home, Abbotsford, are a lock of Prince Charlie's hair, Rob Roy's dirk and a piece of oatcake found on a Highlander's body at Culloden.

Shown opposite is the Courthouse where, in 1793, Sir Walter first appeared as an advocate in a criminal case.

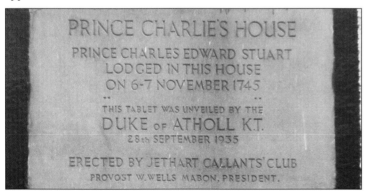

Blackhills Close

40

Prince Charlie's House at Jedburgh, tablet affixed to wall.

Sir Walter Scott & Jedburgh Courthouse

BRAMPTON - THE MARCH CONTINUES

Enroute south Charles stayed at 20 High Cross Street (now a shoe shop) in Brampton. This was his headquarters during the siege of Carlisle from November 12 to 18 1745 and it was here that he received the keys to the city from the mayor of Carlisle. The house is known as Prince Charlie's House.

The Prince also stayed overnight at the George Hotel (formerly the George and Dragon Inn) in Penrith on his long march south.

Shown on the right is 20 High Cross Street Brampton and the George Hotel in Penrith.

The plaque recording his visit to the former is shown below.

PRINCE CHARLIE'S HOUSE

THIS BUILDING
DATES FROM THE YEAR 1603.

IN 1745 'BONNIE' PRINCE CHARLIE
ESTABLISHED HIS HEADQUARTERS HERE
DURING THE SIEGE OF CARLISLE ON
NOVEMBER 12th TO 18th 1745.

20 High Cross Street, Brampton

PENRITH

The George & Dragon Inn, Penrith.

SCOTCH GATE, CARLISLE

When the mayor handed over the keys of Carlisle to Bonnie Prince Charlie it gave Charles and the Jacobites a significant boost as Carlisle was a frontier town of considerable importance.

However when news reached the troops that a government army was in Scotland sadly for the Prince a number of the men defected, returning home to protect their families. Morale was also dealt a blow when there was a temporary falling out between Charles and Lord George Murray.

Nevertheless despite the reduced number of troops Charles insisted on marching on.

After Carlisle was recaptured, much later, by the Duke of Cumberland the fortifications were demolished and it became a Debtors Prison.

Scotch Gate (reconstruction)

Bonnie Prince Charlie seizes Swarkestone Bridge

Swarkestone Bridge crosses the River Trent between the villages of Swarkestone and Stanton by Bridge about 6 miles south of Derby.

It was here on the eve of 4th December 1745 that an event of historical significance took place. The Young Pretender had marched south from Scotland with his army and had taken up residence at Exeter House in Derby. It was there that with his principal officers he discussed arrangements for his triumphal entry into London. That night his men seized Swarkestone Bridge thus securing the principal route south to London. The Virgin's Inn in Derby is understood to have been the prince's headquarters.

The Retreat Begins

Swarkestone Bridge turned out to be the farthest point south reached by Charles and his army as he reluctantly agreed to his officers' pleadings to turn back or face overwhelming odds on reaching the outskirts of London. Lack of English support was part of the problem. Shown here is the cairn erected by the Charles Edward Stuart Society and Marston's Brewery on the 250th Anniversary of the Battle.

The men seizing the bridge included Atholl's Brigade, The Duke of Perth's, Ogilvy's, John Roy Stuart's, Glenbucket's, The Manchester Regiment, Clanranald's, Keppoch's, Appin, Lochiel's, Cluny's, Pitsligo's and Glengarry.

Annually on the anniversary of the occasion the Derby Heritage Society re-enact the storming of the bridge, later retiring to the Hotel for refreshments.

The Bridge and Causeway which date from the 13th century and linked Derby and Coventry is just under one mile long and is the longest stone bridge in England. It featured in the English Civil War being defended by the Royalists against the Parliamentarians.

The Commemorative Cairn

The Hotel and the Cairn

Swarkestone Bridge

45

THE RETREAT CONTINUES

CLIFTON MOOR

On the Prince's retreat north, a skirmish took place at Clifton Moor just south of Penrith, on 18 December 1745. This was considered to be a Jacobite victory. Led by Prince William Augustus, 1st Duke of Cumberland, son of George II the troopers of Bland's regiment who fell were buried in St Cuthbert's churchyard. A monument was erected in recent years by "The Queen's Royal Hussars". The churchyard and monument are shown here.

What is known as "The Rebel Tree" (shown far right) marks the burial place of the Jacobite soldiers who perished. Shown below is the plate providing the information.

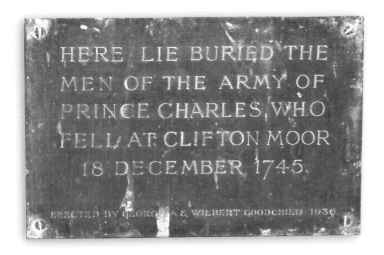

St. Cuthbert's Churchyard with monument in foreground

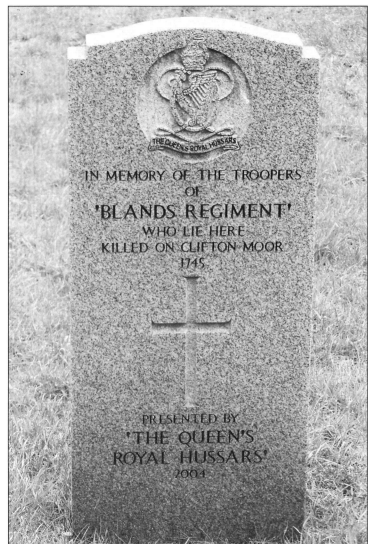

The Bland Monument

The Rebel Tree with plate affixed to fence

HUMPHREY BLAND (1686 – 1763)

Humphrey Bland, British Army General, was not only involved at Clifton Moor but it was he who commanded the government cavalry at the Battle of Culloden. Here is a document signed Hum. Bland in 1751, to the Board of Ordnance. Bland certifies that the last supply of ammunition has been used up by his Regiment of Dragoons. Noted on the document is the subsequent provision of a further supply of 3.5 barrels of corned gunpowder. In 1753 he took over from Albemarle as Commander in Chief in Scotland.

THE DUKE OF CUMBERLAND

Shown far right is Townend Cottage Clifton Moor, where the Duke of Cumberland stayed on the night of the battle of Clifton Moor.

Townend Cottage, Clifton Moor

THE BATTLE OF FALKIRK

North of the border Charles's retreat was via Dumfries and Glasgow. In both places he found hostility rather than support. After some success at Stirling, the Jacobite army had further success at Falkirk. Although possibly indecisive the King's troops under General Hawley lost many men.

THE BATTLE OF CULLODEN

Retreating further into the highlands Charles made his last stand at the Battle of Culloden on 16 April 1746, suffering a heavy and total defeat at the hands of the Duke of Cumberland.

A major reason for his defeat was the Prince's failure to accept the expert advice offered by his experienced Lieutenant General Lord George Murray. His obstinacy extended to choice of location for the battle and the battle plans in general.

When the respective armies met up at Drummossie Moor the Prince's troops were starving, disorganised, outmanoeuvred and outnumbered. He was short of cavalry. Cumberland's men were well fed, well trained regulars with much superior firepower. The fighting lasted for less than an hour. After the defeat at Prestonpans George II had sent a strong force, under General Wade, to Scotland to deal with the Jacobite threat and with limited casualties this was achieved under Cumberland.

FLORA MACDONALD

Charles escaped into the Highlands after Culloden with a ransom of £30,000 on his head and despite the biggest manhunt in history no one betrayed him. He was assisted – over the sea to Skye – disguised as an Irish maid, Betty Burke – by the legendary Flora MacDonald. Supporters then helped Charles escape to France.

Late in 1746, Flora was arrested and taken as a prisoner to Dunstaffnage Castle in Argyll before being transported to the Tower of London. In 1747, Flora was released having been treated as a celebrity rather than being punished.

THE DUKE OF CUMBERLAND

William (1st Duke of Cumberland) became known as "the Butcher" following the slaughter of prisoners and those escaping after the battle was over. Shown here is a part letter signed "William".

Simon Fraser, 11th Lord Lovat
& Philip, Lord Hardwicke

Simon Fraser, 11th Lord Lovat wasn't known as "Simon the Fox" without good reason. In 1715 he was a supporter of George I and the House of Hanover and an advisor to General Wade. By 1745, however, he had changed sides, was a Jacobite and a supporter of Bonnie Prince Charlie while still pretending to favour the Hanovarians.

After providing troops at Falkirk and Culloden there was no hiding place for "Mr Fox". Although managing to escape after Culloden he was tracked down, captured and taken to London for trial.

It was Philip Yorke, 1st Earl of Hardwicke who presided over the trials of Scottish Jacobite peers after Culloden. By 1745, Yorke had become Lord Chief Justice, Privy Councillor and Lord Chancellor.

Lord Lovat was impeached for High Treason and put on trial in Westminster Hall. Finding Lovat guilty, Hardwicke ordered him to be beheaded, hung drawn and quartered, making him the last man to be publicly beheaded in England.

The execution of Lord Lovat was not without farce, scaffolding erected for viewing purposes collapsing and causing the deaths of 20 spectators. Lord Lovat was much amused thus giving rise to the saying "laughing your head off".

Lord Hardwicke's speech giving judgement against Simon Lord Lovat was published and printed by order of the House of Peers. Hardwicke was a signatory to the document shown opposite, issued by William, Duke of Cumberland, in relation to His Majesty's 13th Regiment of Foot.

The Duke of Cumberland

Memorial stones on Culloden battlefield, all to be found in the vicinity of the Cairn (see opposite)

The Memorial Cairn to the clan dead

Leanoch Cottage, between government battle lines

The 2nd Earl of Albemarle

The 2nd Earl of Albemarle, (Willem Annevan Keppel 1702 – 54) commanded the government front line at Culloden, having already been in charge of the government troops at Falkirk, later becoming Commander in Chief in Scotland. He regretted not capturing Bonnie Prince Charlie. In this document of December 1736 he writes to Adair concerning various individuals, mentions Jones for Second Lieutenant in the Marines and requests a warrant appointing William Hawkes Surgeon's Mate in the King's own Regiment. This document was originally in the Ray Rawlins collection.

The Duke of Cumberland

Also shown here is a rare extensive letter (2 pages) signed by the Duke of Cumberland on 6/4/1748 to Solomon Dayrolles, H M Resident in the Hague discussing the payment of £83,000 to the Duke of Wolfenbuttel for the use of his troops.

After Cumberland's cruelty, in Scotland a weed was called "Stinking Billie". In England a flower was called "Sweet William" .

Lieut, Colonel Joseph Yorke

Joseph Yorke, born in 1724, rose rapidly through the ranks to become a Lieutenant – Colonel by 1745. The National Trust for Scotland guide for Culloden (page 47) highlights Yorke's involvement in the 1745 rebellion. In the document shown opposite, The Hague, 6 April 1748, Yorke signs below Cumberland. He later became the British ambassador to the United Provinces.

Dear Adair

I inclose you, Col Peterson's character of Sergt. Abbot of the Marines, he was originaly recomended to me by Sr Edwd. Montague who assured me he was of a very good family. I likewise inclose you a letter from a Qr. Mastr. of Major Regt. to Col. Dalrymple I go out of Town tomorrow morning for five or six days, or would wait upon my Lord Anson to recommend him for a Second Lt. of Marines, if those Commissions are likely to be filled up immediately I must beg of you to mention Dr. Wm. Jones to my Lord Anson in my name. you must be so good as to order a Warrant to be made out for Willm. Hawkes appointing him Surgeons Mate in the Kings own Regt. dated May 30th. I go to Hinchinbrooke to morrow & shall not return 'till Saturday. Yrs my dr Adair

very sincerely

Albemarle

Monday Night

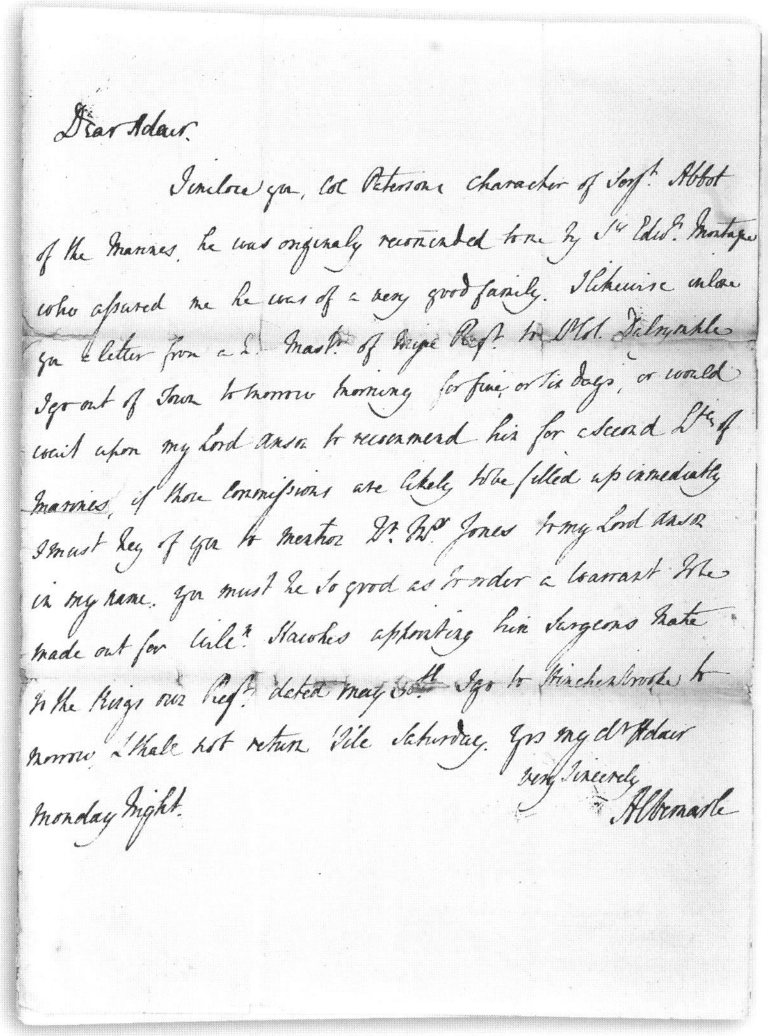

The 2nd Earl of Albemarle

Hague, april 6th n.s. 1748.

Mr Dayrolles, The King's service requiring my immediate departure from this Place, before I could settle with Mons.r Deneken the Wolfenbüttle Minister, what was necessary for the first Payment of the Levy Money allow'd the Duke of Wolfenbüttle for His Troops which enter into the Pay of the Maritime Powers, & as His Majesty has refer'd to me the regulating that affair, provided my stay here would have allowed me; as well as Full Powers to order such Payments to be made for that service as the Treaty specifies; I do hereby, by virtue of that Power, to me given & granted by His Majesty, order & appoint you to settle with Mr Deneken abovemention'd, who is Commission'd on the Part of the Duke of Wolfenbüttle his Master, to receive and give Receipts, for all such Sums of Money as shall be pay'd in consequence of the Convention made with that Prince, and sign'd at the Hague the first of February 1748. N.s.

In

In pursuance of this order, you will give immediate notice to Mr Nicoll His Majesty's Paymaster General of His Forces (at Rotterdam) to issue at your order, the Sum of Eighty three thousand, seven Hundred Florins, Currency of Holland being the first Payment for the Levy Money allow'd for those Troops, and for which you will take Mons.r Deneken's Receipt — Given at the Hague this sixth day of April n.s. 1748.

William.

By His Royal Highness' Command
Joseph Yorke.

To Solomon Dayrolles Esq.r
His Majesty's Resident to
Their High Mightinesses
The States General &c &c &c

The Duke of Cumberland discusses payment for troops.

Lachlan MacLachlan

One of Prince Charles's supporters was Lachlan MacLachlan, 17th Chieftain of the Clan, Castle Lachlan, Argyll.

Shown below is a printed and manuscript receipt for £209.17 shillings received from the Lord Elibank as his supply for his Lands in the shire of Haddington, payable "by virtue of an order from his Royal Highness Charles Prince Regent" signed by Lachlan MacLachlan. There is a further note on the verso signed by Lachlan MacLachlan.

MacLachlan the seventeenth chief of the clan was appointed to the staff of Charles Edward Stuart as commissary - general. He led his clansmen to Edinburgh to join the Prince at Holyrood on 18 September 1745 and fought with him at Prestonpans, Falkirk and Culloden where he was killed.

The name "Elibank" also crops up in relation to a plot or conspiracy to capture the Hanovarian Royal Family. That plot failed around 1752.

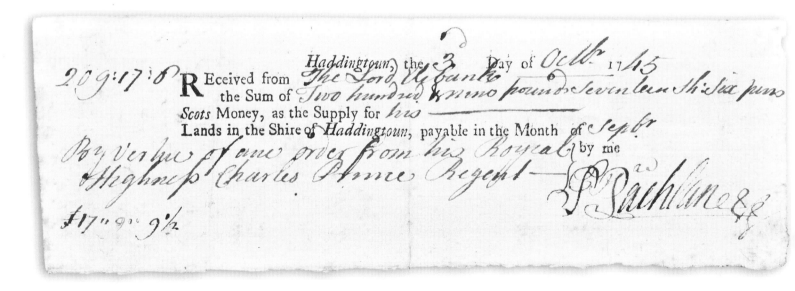

Lord Lewis Gordon

Another major supporter was Lord Lewis Gordon, a naval officer who became a member of the Prince's Council in Edinburgh in October 1745. Gordon recruited for the Prince in Aberdeenshire and Banff and defeated the government force at Inverurie. He commanded his "Lord Lewis Gordon" battalions at the Battles of Falkirk and Culloden. After Culloden he escaped to France.

Shown here is a letter sent by Lord Lewis from Portsmouth, on 21 June 1740. It is "from your most affectionate friend" referring to a cruise Gordon had been on off Cape Finister and the Gallicia Coast and the capture of a privateer with 16 guns, 145 men and two English merchantmen; also asking him to pass on his compliments to all his friends in London including Mr Fairfax and Lady Burlington.

Lady Anne MacKintosh

Enroute to Culloden the prince stayed at Moy Hall, a few miles short of Inverness. Lady Anne MacKintosh who lived there had raised 300 troops in support of Charles and entertained him at Moy Hall. Her husband who was away at the time had also raised troops but in support of the government. This is a good example of how the rebellion had split families.

While the prince was there Lady Anne known as "Colonel Anne" foiled an attempt to capture the prince by strategically placing 5 or 6 members of staff outside and instructing them to make as much noise as possible thus causing the Redcoats to retreat to Inverness.

Dear Sir Portsmouth june 21 1740

This comes to let you know, yt thank God I am well, as I hope this will find all good friends in London, I was intended to have write you, as soon as I came on shoar, but Mr Brooks being to write, by the first post, I thought yt would do as well, we have had a very pleasant cruize, off Cape finister, & ye coast of Gallicia, nothing remarkable happend as, but ye taking of a privateer of 16 guns, & 145 men, & two english merchantmen, taken by him, all which ships are now in Plymouth, as I have nothing more to trouble you with, I shall beg you to give my compliments to all friends & particularly to mr fairfax; & my Lady Burlington, I am Dear Sir your most

affectionate friend,
& humble Servant,
Lewis Gordon

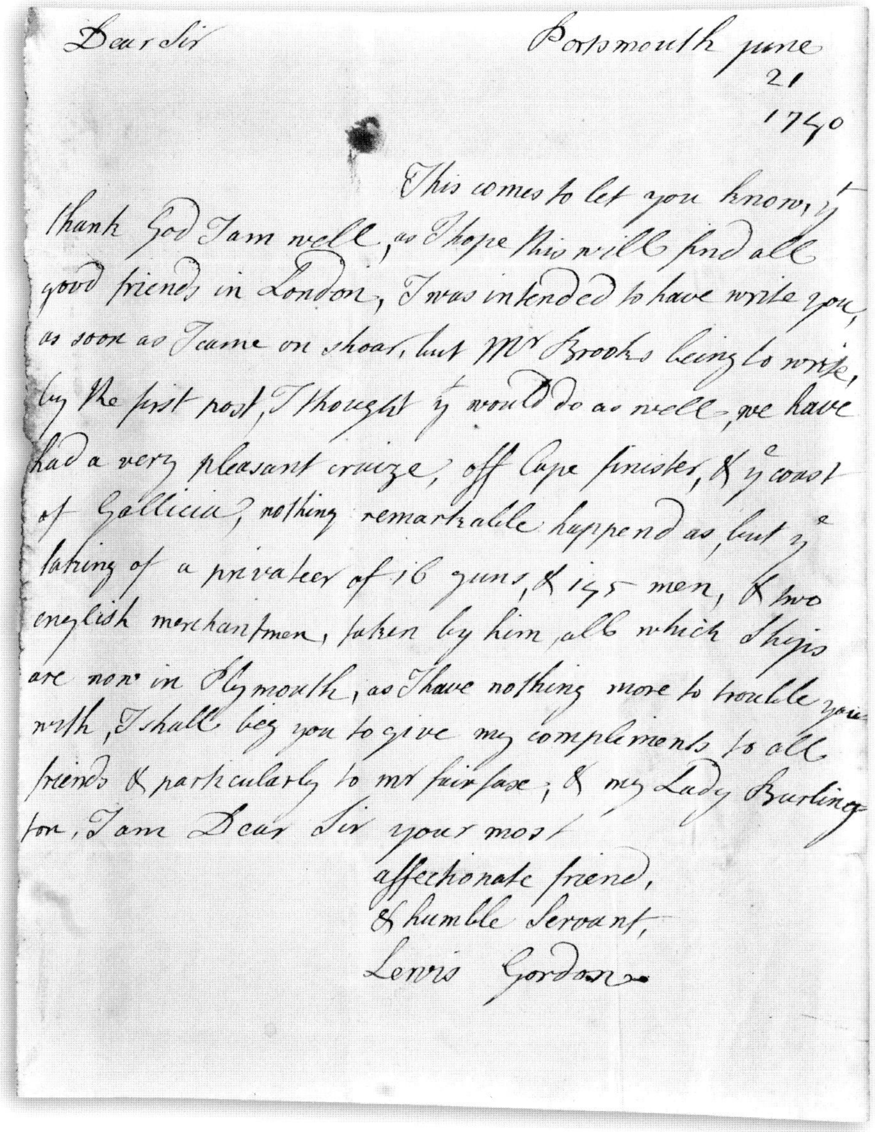

James Barry, 4th Earl of Barrymore

One of the reasons for the failure of the 1745 rebellion was the fact that the promised French support did not arrive. In February 1744, Charles left Dunkirk with thousands of fighting men and ships provided by Louis XV. Before the Royal Navy had to engage with them a storm got up. French boats were sunk and men were lost. The surviving ships including Charles's had to limp back to France.

Involved in the failure was James Barry, the fourth Earl of Barrymore (1667 – 1748), who served as general in the War of the Spanish Succession. He had a political career and was appointed to the Irish privy council in 1714. Late in life he took the impulsive decision to support the Young Pretender, and became a figure of national importance himself when he was discovered as the English rebel who would meet the invading French army in 1744. His advanced age saved him from prosecution and probable execution.

Here is the last page of an autograph letter Signed 'Barrymore', discussing treatments by different doctors, the settlement of a "troublesome affair" in Ireland, and family news.

The Brampton 6

The arm of the law reached far after Culloden. Near Brampton six Jacobites who fought for the Prince were executed by hanging on a capon tree on 21 October 1746. They were James Innes, Patrick Lindsay, Ranald MacDonald, Thomas Park, Peter Taylor and Michael Dellard. The tree has since died and been replaced with a monument erected by the 1745 Association.

Henry Pelham, Prime Minister

After Culloden it was Henry Pelham who had a moderating influence on the treatment of the Jacobites or they would have been treated even more severely. Pelham was really Prime Minister in the years 1743 to 54. Here is a part document of 1746 relating to Lord Widdrington's financial affairs signed by Pelham, Middlesex and Arundell.

Letter (part) signed "Barrymore", London, 4 May 1738

Whereas' by reason of the
carried into the Mint to
Sum of Seven hundred
ice out of the Coinage Duty
ady day 1746 the Sum
ven Pounds and fifteen
s and the extraordinary
and other Charges of the
he said Act to pray and
paying unto William
Majesty's Mint or to his
undred and fifty seven
Imprest and upon Accompt.
nies remaining in the
rvice. And for so doing
l Treasury Chambers

H. Pelham.

Midd lesex

R Arundell

1 & Lord Widdrington's Money

The Brampton 6 Monument   *Prime Minister, Henry Pelham*

59

BONNIE PRINCE CHARLIE

On the run after the battle of Culloden, the Prince resorted to sending letters in cryptic code. Naturally these are difficult to interpret. This is one sent by Charles apparently to a Macdonald, beginning with the statement 'ye two houses by se or Land' and 'attempt far off', enjoins his correspondent to secrecy, mentions the need for funds and the names Gros, Douns and Ryans, and suggests that Ryans, who will write 'immediately [if it is?] on or off', should come in his person with it and give it to Mr Gordon, one page headed 'Munday Morning at 10:1/2', no place or date.

Scholars believe this relates to negotiations for the marriage to Louise. Ryans was Col. Ryan who was involved in them. Funds for her pension were required – the need for funds is mentioned. Gordon is possibly John of the Scots College in Rome.

———————————————

GENERAL GEORGE WADE

George Wade had commanded in Scotland during the 1715 Rebellion following which he built a line of forts to give the government more control in the highlands. The forts were at Fort William, Fort Augustus and Fort George. He was created Field Marshall in 1743 and had a prominent role in the 1745 Rebellion.

Wade is also famous for building roads after the 1745 Rebellion to enable fast deployment of troops with a view to combating any future threats from the north.

Shown opposite is a fine ordnance document signed by Wade and four others 15/11/1742 for equipment to repair HMS Anglesea. Wade's is the highest placed signature at the foot of the second page.

———————————————

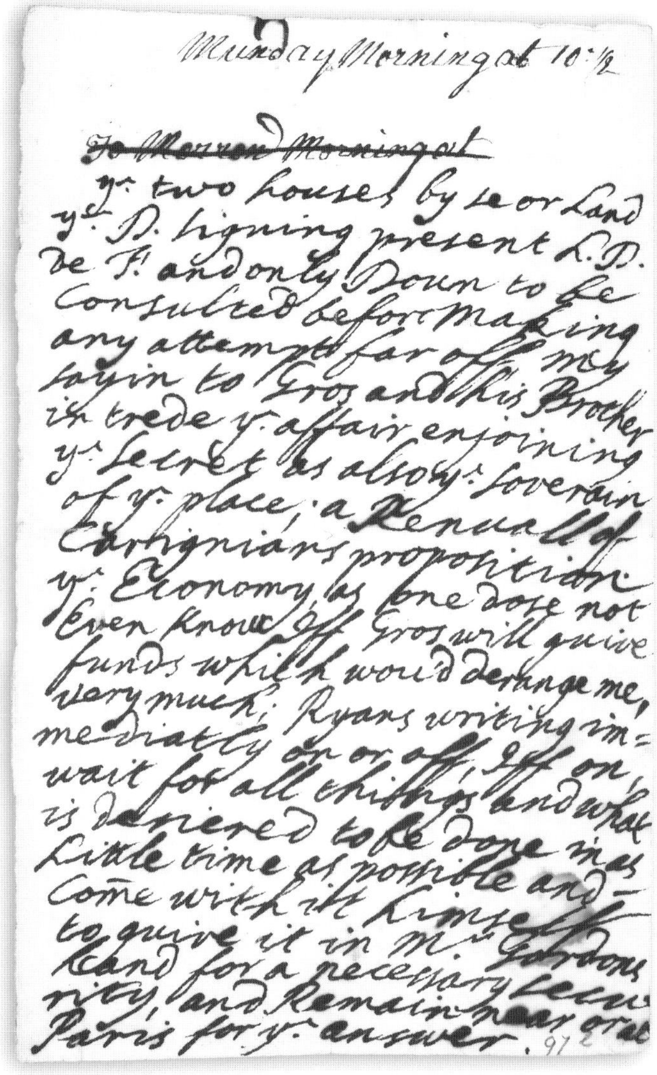

Letter in Cryptic Code

60

Office of Ordnance
15 November 1742

To be forthwith issued out of His Majestys stores within the said office at the Tower the Particulars Undermentioned being for supply And furnishing his Majestys ship the Anglesea lately rebuilt at Hull and ordered to be fitted out there for Channel service by Order of the Board dated the 2 instant —

Axletrees	18 Pounder	0 : 0		
	9	0 : 0		
	6	0 : 0		
Trucks pain	18 Pounder	0 : 0		Woolwich
	9	0 : 0		
	6	0 : 0		
Beds & Coins	18 Pounder	23 : 40		
	9	23 : 40		
	6	5 : 0		
Paper Cartridges	18 Pounder	500		
	9	600		
	6	190		
Sheets of Cartridge Paper	18 Pounder	700		
	9	800		
	6	160		
Formers	18 Pounder	1		
	9	1		

Ladle hooks	p[er]	10	
Linchpins	p[er]	20	
Forelocheys	p[er]	70	
Pen Maul		1	
Spikes	10½ Inches	40	
	9	40	
Nails	30 d	125	
	20 d	125	
	10 d	200	
	6 d	300	
Baskets		12	
Tarr'd rope	5 Inches	0 : 90	
	4	0 : 33	
	2	13 : 0	
Spare Blocks	8 Inches	8	
for Tackles	6½	17	
Tackles Hooks Large	p[er]	11	
Tallow		1 : 0 : 0	
Marlin	skains	20	
Melting Ladles		1	
Sweet oyl	Gallons	8	
Fine paper	quire	10 : 10	
Funnel of Plate		1	
Shott	Musquet	6 : 0 : 0	
	Pistol	0 : 3 : 14	
Pole axes		35	
Swords		100	
Belts		100	
Armourers Tools		1 Sett Compl[eat]	
Chest for Ditto		1	
Padlock and Key for Ditto	each	1	

George Wade

Tho Lascelles   Geo Gregory   W R Earle

A Wilkinson

BONNIE PRINCE CHARLIE
WRITES TO KING LOUIS XV

The first six letters shown here were part of a collection of sixteen letters sold at Bloomsbury Auctions, London in 2002. All six are from Paris and are dated between 13 January and 1 May 1747. Following his defeat at Culloden on 17 April 1746 it was the following October before Bonnie Prince Charlie arrived in France.

The six letters are all to King Louis XV or his secretary and from the papers of Marc-Pierre de Voyer de Paulmy, Comte d'Argenson (1696-1764), secretary of state for war 1743-57; by descent in the family. The letters remained in the possession of successive Comtes d'Argenson at the chateau des Ormes until deposited on loan with the University of Poitiers in 1976 when they acquired a small library stamp. They were returned to the family after the death of the last Count in 1999. Certain of the letters have been known to historians from the contemporary copies Charles sent to his father in Rome. The copies form a considerable portion of the Stuart papers purchased in Rome by George IV and now in the Royal Archives in Windsor Castle.

The first two letters included are signed by Prince Charles from Paris on 13th and 14th January 1747. Both are signed "Charles P". Shown here is the three page letter of the 14th to King Louis XV. The letter of the 13th enclosing it is on page 64.

The letter to the King expands on Charles's proposals to mount a further invasion and complains of a general belief in France that his plans are not feasible. He resolves to leave Paris in the light of the current political climate and offers to appoint a representative to negotiate with the King.

Letter to King Louis XV (Page 1)

eu de reponse, pour ma Justification envers
mes Amis Je serai obligé de leur Communiquer, que je n'ai pas manqué de faire
tout ce que dependoit de moi pour leur
service.
Je n'ai a presenter a Votre Majesté
dans ce moment qu'une reconnoissante
impuissante pour les bienfaits que
J'ai reçu d'elle; un jour peut etre je serai
en etat d'en temoigner ma recon=
noissance comme je le dois J'attendrai ce jour avec Empatience.
Mais malgré mes Malheurs, Je croirois
manquer a ce que je dois aux fidels Sujets de mon Pere et a moi meme si occupé
ici d'un traitement personel je les flattois de l'esperance vaine et eloignée —
de me revoir a leur tete; Je n'ai de ressources a esperer que dans leurs cours, et puisque J'ai eu le bonheur d'eprouver leur
Zele et leur Affection, je tacherai de
me les conserver en perdant Jamais de
veu leurs interets, et en me pretant a
toutes les demarches qu'ils exigeront
de moi, pour les soustraire au joug
dont ils cherchent a s'affranchir.
Je ne puis pas me dispenser d'informer
Votre Majesté de combien il est flatteur pour moi, apres le mauvais succes
de mon Entreprise de recevoir de Compliments de Condoleance pleins d'affeissés, de la part de mes Amis en Angleterre
par une personne de distinction qui
vient d'arriver de ce pays la pour cet
effet, netant chargé de rien aupres les
Ministres de Votre Majesté, et comme
la situation presente ou je me vois

dans Paris, ne paroit pas repondre a la bonté
et l'accueil avec lequel Votre Majesté
m'a reçu a Fountainebleau, dont elle a
J'en suis persuadé de bonnes raisons
connoissant son bon coeur envers moi,
crainte qu'elle ne peut etre interpreté
d'une maniere defavorable a l'honneur
de Votre Majesté et plus encore pour
moi, Je me flatte qu'elle ne desapprouvera pas La resolution que je crois devoir prendre, de me retirer en quelque
lieu ou ma Condition ne tirera pas a
consequence, et ou Je serai toujours pret
a Concourir avec Votre Majesté dans
toutes les Demarches, qui tendront a sa
gloire, et au retablissement de ma Maison dans leurs Justs Droits. Si pendant
mon absence il conviendroit aux interets de Votre Majesté de penser serieusement a une Expedition, pour ces effets,
aussitot que sa Volonté me sera Communiqué, Je reviendrai moi-meme a la
Cour Si Votre Majesté le juge a propos,
ou je nommerai une personne, qui seul
aura ma Confiance, et qui sera uniquement en droit de traitter pour moi aupres de Votre Majesté et ses Ministres.
J'ai l'honneur d'etre,

Monsieur Mon Frere et Cousin
De Votre Majesté
Le bon Frere et Cousin
Charles. P.

A Paris ce 14.
Janvier 1747.

Letter to King Louis XV (Pages 2 & 3)

Letter of 13 January 1747 to Comte d'Argenson

A Paris ce 13, Janvier, 1747.

vep. le 15.

Je vous prie Monsieur de rendre l'inclu a sa majeste. Je prens cette Occasion de Vous renouveller ma reconessance de toutes les politesses que Vous m'avez faites, et de vous assurer en meme tems de mon Amitie,

Votre bon Ami

Charles. P.

Two unsigned letters of 27 March 1747 to Comte d'Argenson

The next two letters are autograph notes to Comte D'Argenson both Paris 27 March 1747 giving an address and false name for communications and asking for the Count's address, the bearer is Monsieur Sheridan (nephew of Sir Thomas Sheridan) who can be trusted to follow any instructions.

Letters from Prince Charles (Cont'd)

Under constant surveillance from British government agents Charles was used to conducting diplomatic negotiations in a cloak-and-dagger atmosphere, here using the address of John Waters and Son, Paris bankers to the Stuarts. The context of these notes, unsigned for obvious reasons, is explained in a letter of 10 April to his father now in the Stuart Papers. "I have received a civill note from Count D'Argenson in which he desiers I should give him an address by which he can always be able to communicate to me his masters pleasure without its ever being suspected, which I did, giving him a cant name to be sent under cover to Waters junior, so that everything is at their door. (Quoted by David Daiches in "Charles Edward Stuart", 1973)

The two unsigned letters of 27 March 1747 to Comte d'Argenson

LETTERS FROM PRINCE CHARLES (CONT'D)

The final two letters to Comte d'Argenson are shown here. These are followed by one in cryptic code.

In the letter dated 23 April 1747 Charles is despondent that he sees no prospect of action across the water and offering his services as aide-de-campe to the King, endorsed in the top margin by d'Argenson noting that the King declined the offer; the other dated 1 May 1747 conveys his profound appreciation of his Majesty's kind words.

Charles's requests for help to mount a third rebellion were turned down by Louis XV as he was in the process of making peace with George II. The Treaty of Aix-La-Chappelle was signed in 1748 recognising the Hanovarian succession.

LETTER IN CRYPTIC CODE

This letter, unsigned, is to do with Charles's financial affairs. It takes the form of a list headed 1747 with various instructions in code. It refers to "John Lambert" and "Waters" his bankers in Paris, "Vignion" presumably Avignon where he spent part of his exile. "Gordon" possibly John Gordon, Rector of the Scots College at Paris and "ye Linnin". Naturally letters of this nature are difficult to understand.

Letter of 23 April 1747

Paris Le 1er May, 1747.

Je receu Monsieur Votre Obli-
gent Lettre de hier et suis pe-
netré des expressions de Bonté
que S. M. S. C. veut bien me faire
je me flatte de La Continuation
de son Amitié Come aussi de
Lui etre un jours utille, quoi
que je le m'alheur apresent de
ne le point etre.

Votre bon Ami,

Charles. P.

Count d'Argenson,

1747. 4 £ 5 s. £ 52 spent.
y. J. P. to draw on Waters,
M. D. to know from Gordon
y. Son Book, y. Wine
y. Silver for 25 Louis
y. Servant to be German
y. detail of all y. rents
with y. form used by J. W.
to receive them, on the
matter I can make one.
y. of fair of Vignon &
y. interest of 5 per c.
all to be put in Elier
having y. acquittances
as also y. Ordonances to
be guiven imediatly
for y. amount of 102 J.
y. Linnin that is not
to be seen how to wash.
If G. knows a gentilman.

Letter of 1 May 1747   *Letter in Cryptic Code*

67

Black Letter Acts

After the 1745 Rebellion

As happened after the First Jacobite rebellion Parliament passed Acts after the 1745 rebellion with a view to controlling the Jacobites and preventing future rebellions. The provisions of two of these Acts are shown below.

(1) The Act of 18.11.1746 (shown here) was passed removing the Estates of certain traitors and for discovering the same. The act sealed the future of the rebels who followed Bonnie Prince Charlie on his adventure which ended at Culloden.

(2) The Act of 17.01.1750 was passed for laying out, making and keeping in repair a proper road for the passage of troops and carriages from Carlisle to Newcastle. George Wade (referred to earlier) used vast sections of Hadrian's wall to do this. The highland army had been able to reach Derby quickly in 1745.

George Wade also transformed the royal barracks at Fort William, Fort Augustus and Fort George.

An act of 1746 also banned the wearing of tartan, the ownership of weapons was banned and the rights of clan chiefs were abolished. In this context it is interesting to note that over 200 years earlier James V was the first member of the Royal family to wear tartan.

King Louis XV appoints a 2nd Lieutenant

Attached is a 1746 Military recommendation signed by King Louis XV and countersigned by Voyer d'Argenson. It promotes Ensign Hasenkampf to 2nd Lieutenant and is dated Fontainbleu, 12 November 1746.

Black Letter Act of 18-11-1746

68

Mons.r Le C.te de Sparre ayant donné a Hasemkampf Enseigne réformé la charge de Lieutenant en second en la Comp.ie de nouvelle levée de Hilleberg dans mon reg.t d'Alfuedois que vous Commandez

je vous Écris cette lettre pour vous dire que vous ayiez a le recevoir et faire reconnoître en lad.e charge de tous ceux, et ainsy qu'il apartiendra, et la présente n'estant pour autre fin, je prie Dieu qu'il vous ayt Mons.r Le C.te de Sparre en sa S.te garde, Écrit a Fontainebleau Le Douze Novembre 1746.

Louis

King Louis XV appoints a 2nd Lieutenant on 12 November 1746

69

FLORA MacDONALD AND DUNSTAFFNAGE CASTLE, ARGYLL

Flora MacDonald was arrested late in 1746 and taken as a prisoner to Dunstaffnage before being transported to the Tower of London. Rather than being punished Flora was allowed to become quite a celebrity. After her release and marriage she and her husband emigrated to North Carolina, her husband fighting on the British side during the American Wars of Independence. After finally returning to Scotland and settling on Skye, Flora died there in 1790.

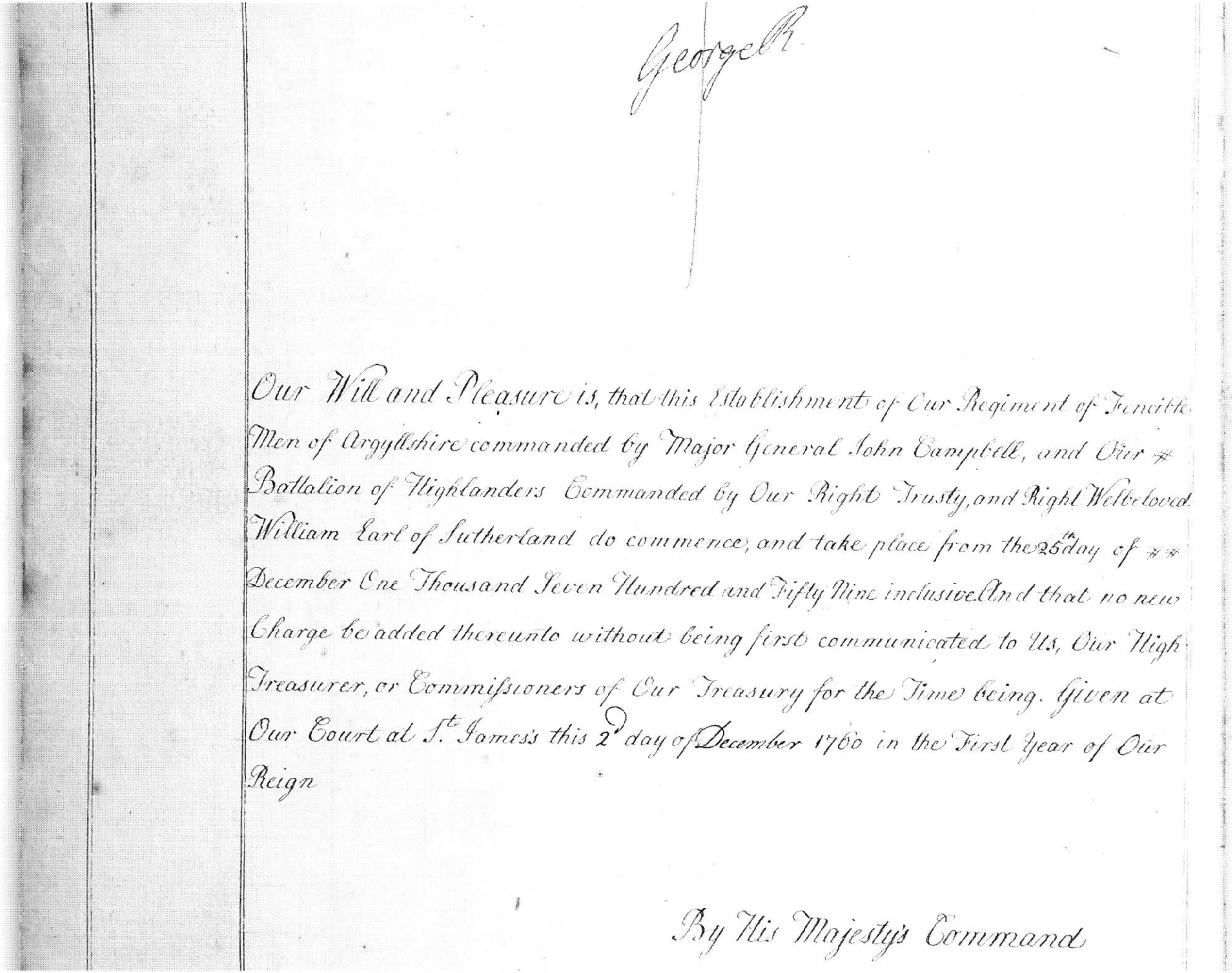

George R.

Our Will and Pleasure is, that this Establishment of Our Regiment of Fencible Men of Argyllshire commanded by Major General John Campbell, and Our Battalion of Highlanders Commanded by Our Right Trusty, and Right Welbeloved William Earl of Sutherland do commence, and take place from the 25th day of December One Thousand Seven Hundred and Fifty Nine inclusive. And that no new Charge be added thereunto without being first communicated to Us, Our High Treasurer, or Commissioners of Our Treasury for the Time being. Given at Our Court at St. James's this 2d day of December 1760 in the First Year of Our Reign

By His Majesty's Command

The Aftermath of the Rebellions - the British government encouraged the creation of fencible regiments to protect it's own shores. As the Jacobites had drawn support from abroad no doubt they were included in this planning. The Argyll and Sutherland Fencibles were the first to be formed and the warrant of 2nd December 1760, signed by George III, is shown here.

CHARLES AS JACOBITE KING CHARLES III

The following two letters are signed by the Young Pretender but as "Charles R" because it is after the death of his father. This letter in English is to the Count of Serrant, Rome 18 February 1766. It acknowledges the Count's condolences on the death of James III on 1 January 1766 and refers to the large packet he sent to Serrant on 4th instant, longs to hear of Serant's safe arrival in Madrid and the success of his negotiations.

Finally he states that what is important to him in his present situation is to have the support of Spain.

His father's death appeared to be Charles's best hope of gaining the Pope's recognition of his claim to the throne occupied by George II and the support of Spain for that purpose but to his mortification Benedict XIV rejected his appeal.

Letter to the Count of Serrant

Rome, February 18th, 1766.

I have received your letter of the 28th past from Montpelier, and heartily thank you for your compliment of condolence on the death of the King my father. Ever sensible of your zealous attachment to my person and service, it will always give me a real satisfaction when I can bestow on you marks of my particular esteem. I sent you a large packet, under M. Joyes's cover, the 4th instant, and to which I refer. Nothing material has since occurred. I shall long to hear of your safe arrival at Madrid, and the success of your negotiation. You know of what importance it is to me to be supported, especially in my present situation, by the court of Spain.

Your sincere Friend
Charles R.

For the Comte de Serrant.

CHARLES AS JACOBITE KING
CHARLES III

The second letter signed Florence 7 March 1775 to the Duke of Melfort in French is thanking him for his prayers. The signature is the one used by Ray Rawlins in his book Four Hundred Years of British Autographs 1970. The document was sold off as part of his collection in June 1980, bought by Maggs Bros.

Like all the documents in this book the letter now forms part of the author's collection.

———————

Included are 14 pages written and/or signed by Prince Charles including his divorce settlement (pages 76 and 77) signed "Charles Comte d'Albanie".

———————

Letter to the Duke of Melfort

Monsieur mon cousin le Duc de Melfort, J'ai reçue avec plaisir vôtre lettre du commencement de cette année, et Je vous remercie des voeux que vous y faites au Ciel pour ma felicité et la conservation de ma personne; Je connois toute la sincerité de vôtre Loyauté, et de votre Zele pour mes interests, ce sont des sentimens hereditaires dans vôtre maison, qui vous assureront toujours ma protection et estime.

Votre Affectionné Cousin

Florence Le 7. Mars, 1775.

Charles. R.

Duc de Melfort.

73

Louise, Countess of Albany

In 1772 Charles married princess Louise of Stolberg. He was 52 years of age and she was only 19.

After their marriage Louise and the Prince lived in Rome, then Florence, but were legally separated in 1784. After the Prince's death she kept court in Florence, accompanied by the Italian poet and dramatist Count Alfieri (d.1803), with nightly receptions in her house on the Lung'arno for men of science and letters.

Shown here are two letters sent by Charles's wife Louise the Countess of Albany. With effect from 1777 Charles had styled himself Count of Albany. The first letter is to Lady Hardy n.p. 27 May n.y. and the second one to Giuseppe Aquari at Rome, sending "infinite thanks for your prayers for me at the start of this new year", on her part "I...will not fail to speak with Cardinal Consalvi on an appropriate occasion about your son. Do not doubt my urgent desire to help you", Florence post mark 9th January n.y.,c.1820.

Consalvi (1757-1824, Pius VII's 'Prime Minister'), was an old friend.

He attracted the notice of Louise's brother-in-law, Cardinal York, when a pupil at the college founded by him at Frascati. A moderate traditionalist, he helped preserve the Papacy through the Napoleonic period, while rooting out many ancient abuses.

J'ai été bien peinée ma très chère Lady en voyant que vous êtes venue chez moi, c'était le moment que je faisais mes fomentations à ma jambe, ce qui m'arrive ordinairement à une heure et demie. Cependant demain il y a relache de [illegible] si vous pouvez me dédommager vous me ferez grand plaisir. Je vous embrasse tendrement et je suis votre dévouée
Louisa d'Albany
le 27 mai à 3 heures

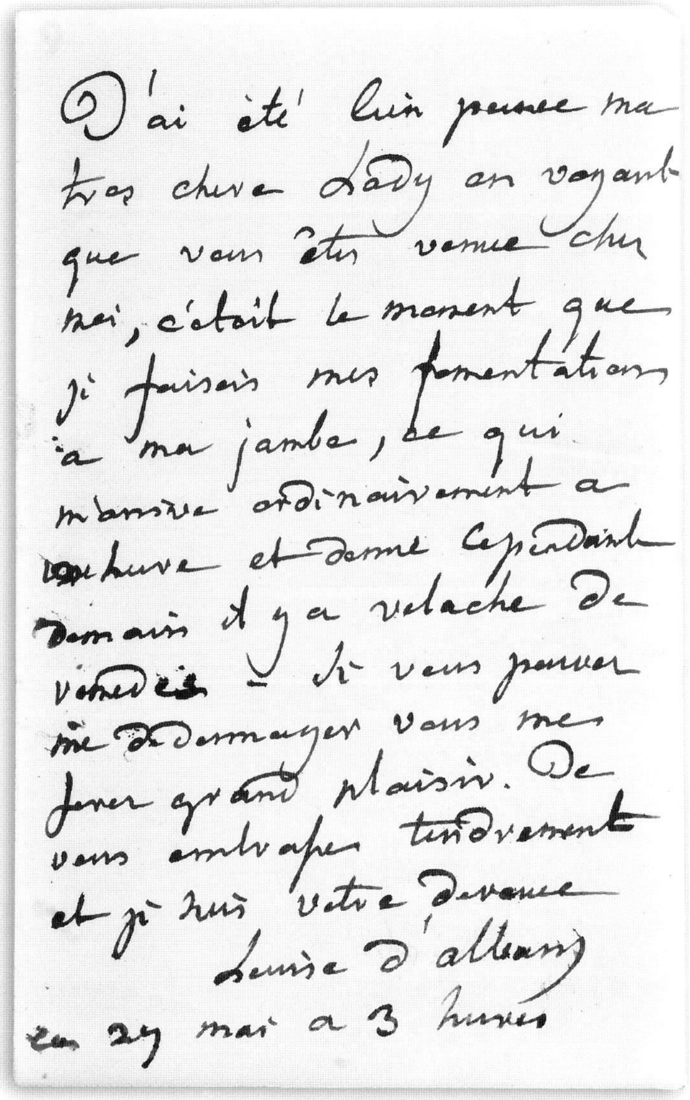

Letter to Lady Hardy

Di dì 9 Gennaio

Ho ricevuta Signor Gioseppe la Sua lettera la ringrazio infinitamente dai voti che ella fa per me al principio di quest'anno, gli auguri' anche a Lei tutto quello che può desiderare faro' Dacconto mia quello che potrò esserle grato e non mancherò di parlare al Signor Cardinale Consalvi del occasione favorevole di Suo figlio non dubita della mia premura ad esserle utile e Benchè mero Luisa di Stolberg Contessa D'Albany

Letter from Louise, Countess of Albany to Giuseppe Aquari

BONNIE PRINCE CHARLIE
SIGNS HIS DIVORCE SETTLEMENT

The paperwork pertaining to the legal separation of Bonnie Prince Charlie and Louise, Countess of Albany extends to six documents comprising 27 pages. Two pages of the most significant document are signed by Charles. Both are signed with a very shaky hand "Comte d'Albanie". In HMC the document is described as Lord Braye's MSS, the Stuart MSS, September 27, 1786.

In this original power in French, executed by Charles before the Chancellor of the French Consulate at Rome, he empowers M Busoni in the presence of or acting with the advice of Mons. J B Vulpian to execute along with the Countess of Albany or her representative the agreement of which a draft is subjoined and to which the seal of the French consulate at Rome is affixed.

The agreement after reciting the securing of the jointure of 40,000 and the pin-money of 12 livres by the marriage contract, the letter of April 1772, the letter of separation of April 3, 1774, the grant by Louis XVI of a pension of 60,000 francs to the Countess of Albany and of the same sum to Charles Edward, and the claim of the Countess to the jointure secured by the contract in addition to the pension of 60,000 francs, whereas her husband contended that the contract had been satisfied by the grant of the pension, witnesses that the Countess agrees to accept a reduced jointure of 20,000 livres charged on all the property of her husband and redeemable at anytime after a year from his decease at her option for 500,000 livres.

Charles signs the agreement.

Nous Louis Dominique Digne
Conseiller Secretaire du Roy, Garde de Ses Archives,
Consul de France à Rome &c

Certiffions et attestons à tous ceux qu'il appartiendra que
Le Sieur Mora qui a Signé L'acte de L'autre part
est Chancelier de Notre Consulat, et qu'en cette qualité
foi entière doit être ajoutée à Ses Actes et Signatures tant
en jugement que dehors: En foi de quoi Nous avons Signé
La presente et icelle fait apposer Le Sceau Royal de
Notre Consulat; à Rome Le Vingt Sept Septembre
Mil Sept Cent Quatre Vingt Six /.

Digne

ma dite Dame pourra exiger Le dit remboursement à Sa volonté,
et Sans aucun autre Delai; 3° qu'au moyen des dits payment et
remboursement, et des presents arrangements et Conventions l'execution
de La Clause du Contract de Mariage du 26 Mars 1772 concernant
Le Douaire et La pension d'entretien, Sera et demeurera irrevocablement
fixée; Comme aussi que L'acte fait et remis Le jour et avant La
Celebration du Mariage, Sera et demeurera revoqué et comme
non avenu, ainsi que tous autres Semblables Actes ou Ecrits relatifs
aux dit Douaire et Pensions; 4° qu'au Surplus l'arrangement
fait par La mediation du Roi de Suede, et fixé à present par
celle de M. Le Comte De Vergennes, Sera Suivi et entierement
executé pendant La vie de mon dit Seigneur Comte d'Albanie;
Enfin qu'au moyen des presentes, et de Leur entiere et parfaite
execution, Mes dits Seigneur et Dame Comte et Comtesse d'Albanie
Seront et demeureront ainsi que Leurs heritiers ou ayant Cause,
respectivement quittes et dechargés de toute Action, Demande
ou pretention, pour raison ou Cause quelconque.
Car ainsi &c /.

J'approuve Le present projet de Transaction; à Rome
Le Vingt Sept Septembre Mil Sept Cent Quatre Vingt Six /.
Charles Comte d'Albanie.

The Seal of The French Consulate is affixed.

Charles "J'approuve le ….. project de Transaction"

BONNIE PRINCE CHARLIE DIES IN 1788

Although Charles did not have a legitimate heir he did have a natural daughter. She was Charlotte Stuart born to his mistress Clementina Walkinshaw. The latter met Charles during the 1745 rebellion and joined him in exile. Charlotte was born in 1753 but in 1760 Clementina left with her.

Many years later Charlotte joined her father who by this time was a disillusioned alcoholic. She was his companion and carer until his death in 1788. Unknown to her father Charlotte had three children to the Archbishop of Cambrai. Just months later, Charlotte also died. In 1784 Charles had recognised Charlotte as his heir, signing a document to that effect. He created her Duchess of Albany.

When Prince Charles Edward Stuart, the Young Pretender died in 1788 the legend, Bonnie Prince Charlie was born. Fuelled by the romanticism of his escape over the sea to Skye with Flora MacDonald and despite his failure at the Battle of Culloden, as the years go by, the legendary status of the boy who was born to be King has grown and will no doubt last forever.

When Charles died of a stroke in 1788, he was buried in the cathedral in Frascati where Henry was Bishop. Henry became Jacobite Henry IX.

HENRY BENEDICT, CARDINAL YORK (1725 – 1807)

Bonnie Prince Charlie is known to have been most displeased when Henry entered the priesthood as a Cardinal since this made the ascendancy of a Stuart to the throne even less acceptable. As Henry IX Henry became the last Stuart claimant to the throne.

Henry was a rich man at one point but after the FRENCH REVOLUTION he was in poverty. He was granted a pension of £4,000 a year by KING GEORGE III and in exchange for this he bequeathed the CROWN JEWELS of ENGLAND to the British Crown. These were the jewels taken by his grandfather James II when he was deposed in 1688.

Here is a letter signed, ('Enico Card le Vescovo') in Italian, to Archpriest Niccolo Seghetti at Frascati, where Henry was Bishop (1761-1803), thanking him for the prompt results of the election of Officers at the Cathedral Chapter on 1st January. He is pleased with their choice, but realises that they may have left the post of First Master of Ceremonies vacant out of respect to him, and "wishing to see...in all things...your Constitutions observed", he desires them to elect one, so that he can grant his approval, Rome, 7th January 1763. [Signed] Henry, Cardinal Bishop.

Cardinal York died in 1807, the last of the Jacobites. A marble tomb financed by King George III for Cardinal York and the two Pretenders was erected at St Peters in Rome in 1819. In the same way as "bloody Mary Tudor" and Mary, Queen of Scots were provided with places of honour in Westminster Abbey, George III was prepared to give recognition to the Jacobite Pretenders in spite of their opposition to his grandfather George II and his father George I.

Cardinal York Medal
Jacobite Henry IX
1788

Sig.r Arciprete Seghetti. Con tutto il maggior piacere ho ricevuto il sollecito avviso ch' Ella ha voluto darmi della seguita elezzione de' nuovi Officiali nel Capitolo tenuto il primo corrente, e L'assicuro essermi riuscita gratissima La scielta de' divisati Soggetti. Ho solamente rilevato La mancanza occorsa di non aver eletto il primo Maestro di Cerimonie; e benchè possa io ciò riferire ad un tratto di cordial rispetto verso di me, pure desiderando veder sempre, ed in tutto, e per tutto osservate Le Loro Costituzioni, bramo, che immediatam.te venghino all'elezzione medesima e poscia me La comunichino, acciò non trovando io su d'essa difficoltà possa venire all'approvazione. Ratifico poi a Lei il mio costante parzial attaccamento, e pregandole dal Cielo ogni bene, resto dando a Lei, ed a tutto il Capitolo colla maggior tenerezza del Cuore La Pastoral Benedizione. Rom.a 7. del 1765.

Errico Card.le Vescovo.

Henry Benedict, Cardinal York writes to Niccolo Seghetti.

FOUR PANELS – FROM THE BATTLE OF PRESTONPANS TAPESTRY

When the author visited Prestonpans and Port Seton it coincided with the exhibition of the magnificent Battle of Prestonpans Tapestry at Cockenzie House. Designed by Andrew Crummy and with the assistance of over 200 volunteers this embroidery of 105 metres does justice to the story of the Battle of Prestonpans. The panels shown here portray the Salutation Hotel, Perth, Bankton House and Holyrood Palace.